KW-169-174

Transport Act 1985

CHAPTER 67

ARRANGEMENT OF SECTIONS

PART I

GENERAL PROVISIONS RELATING TO ROAD PASSENGER TRANSPORT

WITHDRAWN FROM UNIVERSITY OF PLYMOUTH LIBRARY SERVICES

A

PART II

REGULATION OF ROAD PASSENGER TRANSPORT IN LONDON

London local service licences

PART III

THE NATIONAL BUS COMPANY

The Bus Company's disposal programme

PART IV

LOCAL PASSENGER TRANSPORT SERVICES

Passenger Transport Areas

A 2

A 3

A 4

PLYMOUTH POLYTECHNIC
LIBRARY

Accn. No.   **177968**

Class No.   343. 093 GRE.

Contl.   0105467854.

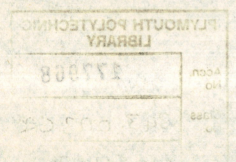

PLYMOUTH POLYTECHNIC
LIBRARY

Accn. No. 477008

Class No.

ELIZABETH II

Transport Act 1985

1985 CHAPTER 67

An Act to amend the law relating to road passenger transport; to make provision for the transfer of the operations of the National Bus Company to the private sector; to provide for the reorganisation of passenger transport in the public sector; to provide for local and central government financial support for certain passenger transport services and travel concessions; to make further provision with respect to the powers of London Regional Transport; to make new provision with respect to the constitution, powers and proceedings of the Transport Tribunal; to make provision with respect to grants payable under section 92 of the Finance Act 1965; to establish a Disabled Persons Transport Advisory Committee; and for connected purposes.   [30th October 1985]

B E IT ENACTED by the Queen's most Excellent Majesty, by and with the advice and consent of the Lords Spiritual and Temporal, and Commons, in this present Parliament assembled, and by the authority of the same, as follows:—

PART I

GENERAL PROVISIONS RELATING TO ROAD PASSENGER TRANSPORT

Abolition of road service licensing

1.—(1) The provisions of Part III of the 1981 Act (road service licences) shall cease to have effect.

Abolition of road service licensing.

(2) Those provisions are replaced—

    (a) in relation to London local services, by Part II of this Act ; and

    (b) in relation to other local services, by sections 6 to 9 of this Act.

(3) Schedule 1 to this Act shall have effect for the purpose of making amendments in other enactments consequential on this section.

Meaning of " local service "

   2.—(1) In this Act " local service " means a service, using one or more public service vehicles, for the carriage of passengers by road at separate fares other than one—

    (a) which is excluded by subsection (4) below ; or

    (b) in relation to which (except in an emergency) one or both of the conditions mentioned in subsection (2) below are met with respect to every passenger using the service.

(2) The conditions are that—

    (a) the place where he is set down is fifteen miles or more, measured in a straight line, from the place where he was taken up ;

    (b) some point on the route between those places is fifteen miles or more, measured in a straight line, from either of those places.

(3) Where a service consists of one or more parts with respect to which one or both of the conditions are met, and one or more parts with respect to which neither of them is met, each of those parts shall be treated as a separate service for the purposes of subsection (1) above.

(4) A service shall not be regarded for the purposes of this Act as a local service if—

    (a) the conditions set out in Part III of Schedule 1 to the 1981 Act (trips organised privately by persons acting independently of vehicle operators, etc.) are met in respect of each journey made by the vehicles used in providing the service ; or

    (b) every vehicle used in providing the service is so used under a permit granted under section 19 of this Act.

(5) Subsections (5)(b), (c) and (6) of section 1 of the 1981 Act (meaning of " fares ") shall apply for the purposes of this section.

Traffic commissioners

3.—(1) There shall cease to be a body of traffic commissioners for each traffic area constituted for the purposes of the 1981 Act (and the appointment of any person who, immediately before the day on which this section comes into force, was a traffic commissioner or deputy to a traffic commissioner shall accordingly come to an end on that day).

Traffic commissioners.

(2) For sections 4 and 5 of the 1981 Act (traffic commissioners) there shall be substituted the following sections—

"Traffic commissioners.

4.—(1) There shall be a commissioner for each traffic area constituted for the purposes of this Act.

(2) The commissioner for each traffic area shall be appointed by the Secretary of State and shall be known as the traffic commissioner for the area.

(3) The traffic commissioner for a traffic area shall be responsible for issuing licences under this Act and shall have such other functions as are given to him by, or in pursuance of, this Act or any other enactment.

(4) Any person appointed to be the traffic commissioner for a traffic area shall—

(a) act under the general directions of the Secretary of State ; and

(b) vacate his office on attaining the age of sixty-five, or on such later date before he attains the age of sixty-six as the Secretary of State may at any time direct, but otherwise hold office during Her Majesty's pleasure.

(5) Where the Secretary of State proposes to appoint a person to be the traffic commissioner for a traffic area he shall, before making the appointment, require that person to declare if he has any, and if so what, financial interest in any transport undertaking which carries passengers or goods by road within Great Britain.

(6) Schedule 2 to this Act shall have effect with respect to traffic commissioners.

Publication of information by traffic commissioners.

5.—(1) Every traffic commissioner shall publish, in such form and at such times as may be prescribed, such information with respect to the exercise, or proposed exercise, of any of his functions under this Act or the Transport Act 1985 as may be prescribed.

(2) Where the traffic commissioner for a traffic area publishes information under this section he shall—

(a) send a copy of the publication—

(i) to every chief officer of police, Passenger Transport Executive and local authority whose area falls partly or wholly within that traffic area ; and

(ii) where that traffic area falls wholly or partly within London, to London Regional Transport ; and

(b) make a copy of it available (by post if required and on payment of such fee as may be prescribed) to anyone who asks for one.

(3) In this section " local authority " means—

(a) in England and Wales, the council of any non-metropolitan county, any district or London borough or the Common Council of the City of London ; and

(b) in Scotland, any regional or islands council."

(3) For Schedule 2 to the 1981 Act (traffic commissioners) there shall be substituted the Schedule set out in Part I of Schedule 2 to this Act.

(4) For subsection (1) of section 59 of the 1968 Act (licensing authority for Part V of that Act) there shall be substituted—

1981 c. 14.

" (1) The traffic commissioner for any traffic area constituted for the purposes of the Public Passenger Vehicles Act 1981 shall exercise the functions conferred on him by this Part of this Act and is in this Part of this Act referred to as " the licensing authority." "

(5) Part II of Schedule 2 to this Act shall have effect for the purpose of making further consequential amendments in other enactments.

Inquiries held by traffic commissioners.

4. For section 54 of the 1981 Act (procedure of traffic commissioners) there shall be substituted the following section—

" Inquiries held by traffic commissioners.

54.—(1) A traffic commissioner may, at such places as appear to him to be convenient, hold such inquiries as he thinks fit in connection with the exercise of his functions.

(2) Where, as respects the proposed exercise of his powers on any occasion, a traffic commissioner re-

ceives a request for an inquiry from two or more persons he may hold a single inquiry in response to those requests.

(3) Subject to any provision made by regulations, any inquiry held under this section shall be public.

(4) Where a traffic commissioner proposes to hold an inquiry for the purpose of considering any application or proposal, he shall publish notice of the inquiry in the prescribed manner.

(5) Where a traffic commissioner holds an inquiry he may, in such circumstances as may be prescribed and subject to any provision made under subsection (6) below, make such order as he thinks fit as to the payment, by such party to the inquiry as he thinks fit, of costs incurred by him or by the Secretary of State in connection with the holding of the inquiry.

(6) Regulations may make provision, in relation to orders under subsection (5) above, as to—

(a) the method of calculating the amount of any costs incurred as mentioned in that subsection ; and

(b) the maximum amount which may be ordered to be paid under such an order.

(7) Any amount so ordered to be paid by any person may be recoverable from him—

(a) in England and Wales, as a debt due to the Crown ; or

(b) in Scotland, by the Secretary of State.

(8) Information with respect to any particular trade or business which is given at any such inquiry while admission to the inquiry is restricted in accordance with regulations shall not be disclosed, so long as that trade or business continues to be carried on, except—

(a) with the consent of the person for the time being carrying it on ;

(b) for the purpose of the discharge by any person of his functions under any enactment mentioned in subsection (9) below ; or

(c) with a view to the institution of, or otherwise for the purposes of, any legal proceedings pursuant to or arising out of any such enactment (including proceedings before the Transport Tribunal) ;

and any person who discloses any information in contravention of this subsection shall be liable on summary conviction to a fine not exceeding level 4 on the standard scale.

(9) The enactments referred to in subsection (8)(*b*) and (*c*) above are—

(*a*) sections 12 to 21 of this Act ; and

(*b*) sections 24 to 28 of the Transport Act 1985.

(10) The Secretary of State may by order made by statutory instrument amend subsection (9) above by adding a reference to an enactment or by removing any such reference ; and any statutory instrument made in exercise of the power conferred by this subsection shall be subject to annulment in pursuance of a resolution of either House of Parliament."

Assistance for traffic commissioners in considering financial questions.

5. After section 17 of the 1981 Act, there shall be inserted the following section—

"Assessors to assist traffic commissioners.

17A.—(1) In considering any financial question which appears to him to arise in relation to the exercise of his functions under section 14, 16 or 17 of this Act, a traffic commissioner may be assisted by an assessor drawn from a panel of persons appointed by the Secretary of State for the purposes of this section.

(2) A traffic commissioner shall pay to any such assessor, in respect of his services, such remuneration as may be determined by the Secretary of State with the consent of the Treasury."

Registration of local services

Registration of local services.

6.—(1) In this section " service " means a local service which is neither a London local service nor a service provided under an agreement with the Railways Board (under section 4A of the 1962 Act) where a railway service has been temporarily interrupted.

(2) Subject to regulations under this section, no service shall be provided in any traffic area in which there is a stopping place for the service unless—

    (*a*) the prescribed particulars of the service have been registered with the traffic commissioner for that area by the operator of the service ;

    (*b*) the period of notice in relation to the registration has expired ; and

    (*c*) the service is operated in accordance with the registered particulars.

(3) In subsection (2) above " the period of notice ", in relation to any registration, means, subject to regulations under this section—

    (*a*) the period prescribed for the purposes of this subsection ; or

    (*b*) if longer, the period beginning with the registration and ending with the date given to the traffic commissioner by the operator as the date on which the service will begin.

(4) An application for registration shall only be accepted from a person who either holds an unconditional PSV operator's licence or a permit under section 22 of this Act or is using, or proposing to use, a school bus belonging to that person for fare-paying passengers in accordance with section 46(1) of the 1981 Act.

(5) In subsection (4) above " unconditional ", in relation to a PSV operator's licence, means a licence which does not have attached to it a condition imposed under section 26(1) of this Act prohibiting, or having the effect of prohibiting, the operator from using vehicles under the licence to provide the service to which the application in question relates.

(6) In this Act any reference to a service registered under this section is a reference to a service in respect of which the prescribed particulars are registered under this section.

(7) Any registration may be varied or cancelled on an application made by the operator of the service to which it relates.

(8) Subject to regulations under this section, the variation or cancellation of a registration shall become effective—

    (*a*) on the expiry of the period beginning with the date on which the traffic commissioner accepts the application and ending with the date determined in accordance with regulations under this section ; or (*b*) if later, on the day given to the traffic commissioner by the operator as the effective date for the variation or (as the case may be) cancellation.

(9) Regulations may be made for the purpose of carrying this section into effect and any such regulations may, in particular, make provision—

  (*a*) for permitting the variation of a registered service, in such circumstances as may be prescribed, without variation of the registration ;

  (*b*) for excluding or modifying the application of subsection (3) or (8) above in such cases or classes of case as may be prescribed ;

  (*c*) that in such cases or classes of case as may be prescribed—

    (i) subsection (2) above shall have effect as if for the reference in paragraph (*b*) to the period of notice there were substituted a reference to such period as the traffic commissioner may determine ;

    (ii) subsection (8) above shall have effect as if for the reference in paragraph (*a*) to the date on which the period mentioned in that paragraph is to expire there were substituted a reference to such date as he may determine ;

  (*d*) as to the procedure for applying for registration or for the variation or cancellation of a registration ;

  (*e*) for an application for registration or for the variation or cancellation of a registration not to be accepted by the traffic commissioner to whom it is made unless the applicant gives to the commissioner such information as he may reasonably require in connection with the application ;

  (*f*) as to the traffic commissioner to whom an application for registration is to be made in the case of services which will run through the areas of two or more traffic commissioners ;

  (*g*) as to the documents (if any) to be issued by a traffic commissioner with respect to registrations ;

  (*h*) as to the cancellation of registrations relating to discontinued services ;

  (*i*) for enabling a traffic commissioner to require the operator of a registered service, in such circumstances as may be prescribed, to keep records of such matters relating to the operation of the service, in such manner, as may be prescribed ;

  (*j*) for requiring the operator of a registered service who is required to keep records by regulations made by virtue of paragraph (*i*) above to make those records available to the traffic commissioner;

(*k*) for requiring the operator or prospective operator of a registered service to give, to such persons and at such times as may be prescribed, such information as may be prescribed with respect to the service, or proposed service, or any proposal to vary or cancel the registration of the service;

(*l*) for excluding from the application of this section services which are—

(i) excursions or tours; or

(ii) excursions or tours falling within a prescribed class.

7.—(1) If a traffic authority asks him to exercise his powers under this section in relation to a particular traffic problem, the traffic commissioner for any traffic area may determine conditions (" traffic regulation conditions ") which must be met in the provision of services in the area to which the conditions are expressed to apply.

Application of traffic regulation conditions to local services subject to registration under section 6.

(2) In this section " service " means any local service to which section 6 of this Act applies.

(3) The area to which traffic regulation conditions may be expressed to apply is any part of the traffic area of the traffic commissioner determining them.

(4) No traffic commissioner shall determine traffic regulation conditions unless he is satisfied, after considering the traffic in the area in question, that such conditions are required in order to—

(*a*) prevent danger to road users; or

(*b*) reduce severe traffic congestion.

(5) In considering what traffic regulation conditions to apply to a particular area a traffic commissioner shall have regard in particular to the interests of—

(*a*) those who have registered under section 6 of this Act services which are or will be operated in the area;

(*b*) those who are, or are likely to be, users of such services; and

(*c*) persons who are elderly or disabled.

(6) The purposes for which traffic regulation conditions may be determined are the regulation of—

(*a*) the routes of services;

(*b*) the stopping places for services;

    (c) when vehicles used in providing services may stop at such stopping places and for how long they may do so ; and

    (d) such other matters as may be prescribed.

(7) Subject to subsection (8) below, traffic regulation conditions shall apply—

    (a) to all services operated in the area to which the conditions are expressed to apply ; or

    (b) to such class of service operated there as may be specified in the conditions.

(8) Where the traffic commissioner for any traffic area is satisfied that traffic regulation conditions applying generally to a particular part of his traffic area would be inappropriate as a means of achieving the regulation of traffic which he considers is required there, he may determine traffic regulation conditions which apply only to the service or services specified in the conditions.

(9) Before determining any traffic regulation conditions, a traffic comissioner shall hold an inquiry if he has received (within the prescribed period) a request for an inquiry from—

    (a) the traffic authority which made the request under subsection (1) above ;

    (b) any other traffic authority likely to be affected by traffic regulation conditions determined in response to that request ; or

    (c) any person who has registered under section 6 of this Act a service which is or will be operated in the area in question ;

and the request has not been withdrawn.

(10) Subsection (9) above shall not apply where the traffic commissioner is satisfied that the conditions should be determined without delay.

(11) Where, in reliance on subsection (10) above, a traffic commissioner determines traffic regulation conditions without first holding an inquiry, he shall hold one as soon as is reasonably practicable if any person mentioned in subsection (9)(a) or (c) above or any other traffic authority affected by the conditions has, before the end of the prescribed period, asked him to do so.

(12) Before asking a traffic commissioner to exercise his powers under this section in relation to a trunk road, a traffic authority shall obtain leave of the Secretary of State ; but leave given under this subsection shall not be taken to indicate the Secretary of State's approval of any conditions determined by the traffic commissioner in response to the request.

(13) Traffic regulation conditions may make different provision with respect to the operation of any service to which they apply during different periods of the year, on different days of the week, or at different times during any period of 24 hours.

(14) A traffic commissioner may vary or revoke any traffic regulation conditions determined by him on being requested to do so by—

(a) any traffic authority ; or

(b) the operator of any service affected by the conditions.

(15) In this section " traffic authority " means—

(a) in relation to England and Wales, the council of any metropolitan district or non-metropolitan county ; and

(b) in relation to Scotland, the council of any region or islands area.

8.—(1) Where traffic regulation conditions have been determined under section 7 of this Act, it shall be the duty of the traffic commissioner by whom any relevant licence or permit has been granted to attach the conditions to that licence or, as the case may be, to that permit. Enforcement of traffic regulation conditions, etc.

(2) In this section—

" licence " means a PSV operator's licence ;

" permit " means a permit under section 22 of this Act ;

and a licence or permit is relevant for the purposes of this section if a local service registered under section 6 of this Act by the holder of the licence or permit is affected by the conditions.

(3) Where the traffic commissioner who determined the traffic regulation conditions and the traffic commissioner who granted the relevant licence or permit are different, it shall be the duty of the commissioner determining the conditions to send to the other commissioner—

(a) details of the conditions ; and

(b) the name of the person registering the particulars of the local service.

(4) If traffic regulation conditions which have been attached to a licence or permit under this section are subsequently varied or revoked, it shall be the duty of the traffic commissioner or commissioners concerned to secure that the conditions as so attached are correspondingly varied or (as the case may be) removed.

(5) Traffic regulation conditions shall be of no effect to the extent to which they are incompatible with any provision made by or under any enactment prohibiting or restricting the use of any road by traffic.

(6) Where the operator of a local service is unable both to operate the service in accordance with the particulars of the service registered under section 6 of this Act and to comply with—

    (a) traffic regulation conditions ; or

    (b) any other provision of a kind mentioned in subsection (5) above ;

any failure to operate the service in accordance with those particulars which occurs at any time before the expiry of the prescribed period beginning with the coming into force of the conditions or provision shall be disregarded to the extent to which it is attributable to his having to comply with the conditions or provision.

Appeals against traffic regulation conditions.

9.—(1) Any person to whom subsection (2) below applies may appeal to the Secretary of State against—

    (a) the determination, variation or revocation of any traffic regulation conditions under section 7 of this Act ; or

    (b) the refusal by a traffic commissioner to comply with a request duly made under that section to determine, vary or revoke any such conditions.

(2) The persons to whom this subsection applies are—

    (a) in relation to any determination, variation or revocation of conditions—

        (i) any person who has registered under section 6 of this Act a local service which is, or is likely to be, affected by them ; and

        (ii) any traffic authority aggrieved by the decision in question ; and

    (b) in relation to any refusal to comply with a request, the person making the request.

(3) An appeal under this section must be made within the prescribed time and in the prescribed manner, and provision may be made by regulations as to the procedure to be followed in connection with such appeals.

(4) On the determination of an appeal under this section, the Secretary of State may confirm, vary or reverse the decision appealed against and may give such directions as he thinks fit to the traffic commissioner for giving effect to his decision.

(5) An appeal lies at the instance of any of the persons mentioned in subsection (6) below on any point of law arising from a decision of the Secretary of State on an appeal under this section—

    (a) to the High Court, where the area of the traffic commissioner concerned is in England or Wales ; and

    (b) to the Court of Session, where it is in Scotland.

(6) The persons who may appeal against any such decision of the Secretary of State are—

(a) the person who appealed to him ;

(b) any person who had a right to appeal to him against the relevant decision of the traffic commissioner but did not exercise that right ;

(c) any traffic authority aggrieved by the decision ; and

(d) the traffic commissioner whose decision was appealed against.

(7) If on an appeal under subsection (5) above the High Court or Court of Session is of opinion that the decision appealed against was erroneous in point of law, it shall remit the matter to the Secretary of State with the opinion of the court for re-hearing and determination by him.

(8) No appeal to the Court of Appeal may be brought from a decision of the High Court under this section except with the leave of the High Court or the Court of Appeal.

(9) An appeal shall lie, with the leave of the Court of Session or the House of Lords, from any decision of the Court of Session under this section ; and such leave may be given on such terms as to costs, expenses or otherwise as the Court of Session or the House of Lords determine.

(10) In this section " traffic authority " has the same meaning as in section 7 of this Act.

Taxis and hire cars

10.—(1) In the circumstances mentioned in subsection (2) below, a licensed taxi may be hired for use for the carriage of passengers for hire or reward at separate fares without thereby—

(a) becoming a public service vehicle for the purposes of the 1981 Act or any related enactment ; or

(b) ceasing (otherwise than by virtue of any provision made under section 13 of this Act) to be subject to the taxi code.

(2) The circumstances are that—

(a) the taxi is hired in an area where a scheme made under this section is in operation ;

(b) the taxi is licensed by the licensing authority for that area ; and

(c) the hiring falls within the terms of the scheme.

(3) In this section "licensing authority " means—

(a) in relation to the London taxi area, the Secretary of State or the holder for the time being of any office

Immediate hiring of taxis at separate fares.

           designated by the Secretary of State for the purposes of this section ; and

      (b) in relation to any other area in England and Wales, the authority having responsibility for licensing taxis in that area.

(4) For the purposes of this section, a licensing authority may make a scheme for their area and shall make such a scheme if the holders of at least ten per cent. of the current taxi licences issued by the authority request the authority in writing to do so.

(5) Any scheme made under this section shall—

      (a) designate the places in the area from which taxis may be hired under the scheme (" authorised places ") ;

      (b) specify the requirements to be met for the purposes of the scheme in relation to the hiring of taxis at separate fares ; and

      (c) if made otherwise than by the Secretary of State—

            (i) include such provision, or provision of such description, as may be prescribed for the purposes of this sub-paragraph ;

            (ii) not include provision of any such description as may be prescribed for the purposes of this sub-paragraph.

(6) Subject to subsection (5) above, any scheme made under this section may, in particular, make provision with respect to—

      (a) fares ;

      (b) the display of any document, plate, mark or sign for indicating an authorised place or that a taxi standing at an authorised place is available for the carriage of passengers at separate fares ;

      (c) the manner in which arrangements are to be made for the carriage of passengers on any such hiring as is mentioned in subsection (1) above ; and

      (d) the conditions to apply to the use of a taxi on any such hiring.

(7) A licensing authority may, subject to subsection (5) above, vary any scheme made by them under this section.

(8) Except in the case of a scheme made by the Secretary of State, any scheme under this section, and any variation of such a scheme, shall be made in accordance with the prescribed procedure.

(9) For the purposes of this section—

      (a) the hiring of a taxi falls within the terms of a scheme if—

            (i) it is hired from an authorised place ; and

(ii) the hiring meets the requirements specified by the licensing authority as those to be met for the purposes of the scheme ; and

(b) a taxi is hired from an authorised place if it is standing at that place when it is hired and the persons hiring it are all present there.

(10) The power of the Secretary of State to make a scheme for the purpose of this section shall be exercisable by order.

11.—(1) Where the conditions mentioned in subsection (2) below are met, a licensed taxi or licensed hire car may be used for the carriage of passengers for hire or reward at separate fares without thereby—

(a) becoming a public service vehicle for the purposes of the 1981 Act or any related enactment ; or

(b) ceasing (otherwise than by virtue of any provision made under section 13 of this Act) to be subject to the taxi code or (as the case may be) the hire car code.

(2) The conditions are that—

(a) all the passengers carried on the occasion in question booked their journeys in advance ; and

(b) each of them consented, when booking his journey, to sharing the use of the vehicle on that occasion with others on the basis that a separate fare would be payable by each passenger for his own journey on that occasion.

12.—(1) Where the holder of a taxi licence—

(a) applies to the appropriate traffic commissioner for a restricted PSV operator's licence to be granted to him under Part II of the 1981 Act ; and

(b) states in his application that he proposes to use one or more licensed taxis to provide a local service ;

section 14 of the 1981 Act (conditions to be met before grant of PSV operator's licence) shall not apply and the commissioner shall grant the application.

(2) In this section " special licence " means a restricted PSV operator's licence granted by virtue of this section.

(3) Section 15 of the 1981 Act (duration of licences) shall apply in relation to any special licence as if it required the duration of the licence to be—

(a) five years ; or

(*b*) where the application for the licence specifies a shorter period, that shorter period.

(4) Without prejudice to his powers to attach other conditions under section 16 of the 1981 Act, any traffic commissioner granting a special licence shall attach to it, under that section, the conditions mentioned in subsection (5) below.

(5) The conditions are—

(*a*) that every vehicle used under the licence shall be one for which the holder of the licence has a taxi licence ; and

(*b*) that no vehicle shall be used under the licence otherwise than for the purpose of providing a local service with one or more stopping places within the area of the authority which granted the taxi licence of the vehicle in question.

(6) In subsection (5)(*b*) above " local service " does not include an excursion or tour.

(7) The maximum number of vehicles which the holder of a special licence may at any one time use under the licence shall be the number of vehicles for which (for the time being) he holds taxi licences ; and a condition to that effect shall be attached to every special licence under section 16(1) of the 1981 Act.

(8) Section 1(2) of the 1981 Act (vehicle used as public service vehicle to be treated as such until that use is permanently discontinued) shall not apply to any use of a licensed taxi for the provision of a local service under a special licence.

(9) At any time when a licensed taxi is being so used it shall carry such documents, plates and marks, in such manner, as may be prescribed.

(10) Such provisions in the taxi code as may be prescribed shall apply in relation to a licensed taxi at any time when it is being so used ; and any such provision may be so applied subject to such modifications as may be prescribed.

(11) For the purposes of section 12(3) of the 1981 Act (which provides that where two or more PSV operators' licences are held they must be granted by traffic commissioners for different traffic areas), special licences shall be disregarded.

(12) A person may hold more than one special licence but shall not at the same time hold more than one such licence granted by the traffic commissioner for a particular traffic area.

(13) The following provisions shall not apply in relation to   PART I
special licences or (as the case may be) the use of vehicles
under such licences—

    (*a*) sections 16(1A) and (2), 17(3)(*d*), 18 to 20, 22 and 26
       of the 1981 Act; and

    (*b*) section 26(5) and (6) of this Act;

and for the purposes of section 12 of that Act this section shall
be treated as if it were in Part II of that Act.

13.—(1) The Secretary of State may by order make such modi- Provisions
fications of the taxi code and the hire car code as he sees fit for supplementary
the purpose of supplementing the provisions of sections 10 to 12 to sections 10
of this Act. to 12.

(2) Any order made under subsection (1) above may, in particular, modify any provision—

    (*a*) relating to fares payable by the hirer of a vehicle;

    (*b*) requiring the driver of any vehicle to accept any hiring,
       or to drive at the direction of a hirer, or (as the case
       may be) of a prospective hirer, to any place within or
       not exceeding any specified distance or for any period
       of time not exceeding a specified period from the time
       of hiring;

    (*c*) making the carriage of additional passengers in any
       vehicle which is currently subject to a hiring dependent
       on the consent of the hirer.

(3) In this section, and in sections 10 to 12 of this Act—

" licensed taxi " means—

        (*a*) in England and Wales, a vehicle licensed
    under—

           (i) section 37 of the Town Police Clauses Act 1847 c. 89.
            1847; or

           (ii) section 6 of the Metropolitan Public Car- 1869 c. 115.
            riage Act 1869;

    or under any similar enactment; and

        (*b*) in Scotland, a taxi licensed under section 10
    of the Civic Government (Scotland) Act 1982;   1982 c. 45.

" London taxi area " means the area to which the Metro-
    politan Public Carriage Act 1869 applies;

" licensed hire car " means a vehicle which is licensed under
    section 48 of the Local Government (Miscellaneous 1976 c. 57.
    Provisions) Act 1976;

" hire car code ", in relation to a licensed hire car used as
    mentioned in section 11 of this Act, means those pro-

visions made by or under any enactment which would apply if it were hired by a single passenger for his exclusive use ;

" related enactment ", in relation to the 1981 Act, means any statutory provision (whenever passed or made) relating to public service vehicles in which " public service vehicle " is defined directly or indirectly by reference to the provisions of the 1981 Act ;

" taxi code ", in relation to any licensed taxi used as mentioned in section 10, 11 or 12 of this Act, means—

> (*a*) in England and Wales, those provisions made by or under any enactment which would apply if the vehicle were plying for hire and were hired by a single passenger for his exclusive use ; and

1982 c. 45.

> (*b*) in Scotland, the provisions of sections 10 to 23 of the Civic Government (Scotland) Act 1982, and Part I of that Act as it applies to these provisions ; and

1869 c. 115.
1847 c. 89.

" taxi licence " means a licence under section 6 of the Metropolitan Public Carriage Act 1869, section 37 of the Town Police Clauses Act 1847 or any similar enactment, or a taxi licence under section 10 of the Civic Government (Scotland) Act 1982.

(4) Any order made under subsection (1) above may contain such supplementary, incidental, consequential and transitional provisions (including provisions modifying any enactment contained in any Act other than this Act) as appear to the Secretary of State to be necessary or expedient in consequence of any modification of the taxi code or the private hire car code made by the order.

Operation of taxis and private hire cars in Scotland for the carriage of passengers at separate fares.

14.—(1) As respects Scotland, a taxi (other than a taxi which is for the time being operating a local service which is or requires to be registered under this Part of this Act, has been previously advertised and has a destination and route which are not entirely at the discretion of the passengers) or private hire car which is used for the carriage of passengers for hire or reward at separate fares shall not by reason of such use become a public service vehicle for the purposes of the 1981 Act or any related enactment.

(2) In this section "taxi" and "private hire car" have the meanings given in section 23 of the Civic Government (Scotland) Act 1982 and " related enactment " has the meaning given in section 13(3) of this Act.

15.—(1) Where, immediately before the commencement of this section, the provisions of the Town Police Clauses Act 1847 with respect to hackney carriages and of the Town Police Clauses Act 1889 (as incorporated in each case in the Public Health Act 1875) were not in force throughout the whole of the area of a district council in England and Wales whose area lies outside the area to which the Metropolitan Public Carriage Act 1869 applies, those provisions (as so incorporated) shall—

PART I
Extension of taxi licensing in England and Wales.
1847 c. 89.
1889 c. 14.
1875 c. 55.
1869 c. 115

   (a) if not then in force in any part of the council's area, apply throughout that area ; and

   (b) if in force in part only of its area, apply also in the remainder of that area.

(2) Where part only of a district council's area lies outside the area to which the Act of 1869 applies, that part shall, for the purposes of subsection (1) above, be treated as being the area of the council.

(3) So much of any local Act as enables a district council to bring to an end the application of the provisions mentioned in subsection (1) above to the whole or any part of their area shall cease to have effect.

16. The provisions of the Town Police Clauses Act 1847 with respect to hackney carriages, as incorporated in any enactment (whenever passed), shall have effect—

Taxi licensing: control of numbers.

   (a) as if in section 37, the words " such number of " and " as they think fit " were omitted ; and

   (b) as if they provided that the grant of a licence may be refused, for the purpose of limiting the number of hackney carriages in respect of which licences are granted, if, but only if, the person authorised to grant licences is satisfied that there is no significant demand for the services of hackney carriages (within the area to which the licence would apply) which is unmet.

17.—(1) In this section—

London taxi and taxi driver licensing: appeals.

   " licence " means a licence under section 6 of the Metropolitan Public Carriage Act 1869 (taxi licences) or under section 8 of that Act (taxi driver licences) ; and

   " licensing authority " means the person empowered to grant a licence.

(2) Where the licensing authority has refused to grant, or has suspended or revoked, a licence the applicant for, or (as the

PART I   case may be) holder of, the licence may, before the expiry of the prescribed period—

     (*a*) require the authority to reconsider his decision ; or

     (*b*) appeal to the appropriate court.

(3) Any call for a reconsideration under subsection (2) above must be made to the licensing authority in writing.

(4) On any reconsideration under this section the person calling for the decision to be reconsidered shall be entitled to be heard either in person or by his representative.

(5) If the person calling for a decision to be reconsidered under this section is dissatisfied with the decision of the licensing authority on reconsideration, he may, before the expiry of the prescribed period, appeal to the appropriate court.

(6) On any appeal to it under this section, the court may make such order as it thinks fit ; and any order which it makes shall be binding on the licensing authority.

(7) Where a person holds a licence which is in force when he applies for a new licence in substitution for it, the existing licence shall continue in force until the application for the new licence, or any appeal under this section in relation to that application, is disposed of, but without prejudice to the exercise in the meantime of any power of the licensing authority to revoke the existing licence.

(8) For the purposes of subsection (7) above, where the licensing authority refuses to grant the new licence the application shall not be treated as disposed of—

     (*a*) where no call for a reconsideration of the authority's decision is made under subsection (2) above, until the expiry of the prescribed period ;

     (*b*) where such a reconsideration is called for, until the expiry of the prescribed period which begins by reference to the decision of the authority on reconsideration.

(9) Where the licensing authority suspends or revokes a licence, or confirms a decision to do so, he may, if the holder of the licence so requests, direct that his decision shall not have effect until the expiry of the prescribed period.

(10) In this section " the appropriate court " means the magistrates' court for the petty sessions area in which the licensing authority has his office or, if he has more than one office, his principal office.

Modification of PSV requirements in relation to vehicles used   PART I
for certain purposes

18. Sections 12(1) and 22 of the 1981 Act (licensing of opera-   Exemption
tors and drivers in relation to the use of public service vehicles   from PSV
for the carriage of passengers) shall not apply—   operator and
       driver
   (a) to the use of any vehicle under a permit granted under   licensing
       section 19 of this Act, if and so long as the require-   requirements
       ments under subsection (2) of that section are met ;   of vehicles
       used under
   (b) to the use of any vehicle under a permit granted under   permits.
       section 22 of this Act ; or
   (c) in relation to the driving of any vehicle at a time when
       it is being used as mentioned in paragraph (a) or (b)
       above.

19.—(1) In this section and sections 20 and 21 of this Act—   Permits in
   " bus " means a vehicle which is adapted to carry more   relation to
       than eight passengers ;   use of buses
       by educational
   " large bus " means a vehicle which is adapted to carry   and other
       more than sixteen passengers ;   bodies.
   " small bus " means a vehicle which is adapted to carry
       more than eight but not more than sixteen passengers ;
       and
   " permit " means a permit granted under this section in
       relation to the use of a bus for carrying passengers
       for hire or reward.

(2) The requirements that must be met in relation to the use
of a bus under a permit for the exemption under section 18(a)
of this Act to apply are that the bus—
   (a) is being used by a body to whom a permit has been
       granted under this section ;
   (b) is not being used for the carriage of members of the
       general public nor with a view to profit nor inciden-
       tally to an activity which is itself carried on with a
       view to profit ;
   (c) is being used in evey respect in accordance with any
       conditions attached to the permit ; and
   (d) is not being used in contravention of any provision of
       regulations made under section 21 of this Act.

(3) A permit in relation to the use of a small bus may be
granted by a body designated by an order under subsection (7)
below either to itself or to any other body to whom, in accordance with the order, it is entitled to grant a permit.

(4) A permit in relation to the use of a small bus may be
granted by a traffic commissioner to any body appearing to him
to be eligible in accordance with subsection (8) below and to be
carrying on in his area an activity which makes it so eligible.

(5) A permit in relation to the use of a large bus may be granted by a traffic commissioner to any body which assists and co-ordinates the activities of bodies within his area which appear to him to be concerned with—

(a) education ;

(b) religion ;

(c) social welfare ; or

(d) other activities of benefit to the community.

(6) A traffic commissioner shall not grant a permit in relation to the use of a large bus unless satisfied that there will be adequate facilities or arrangements for maintaining any bus used under the permit in a fit and serviceable condition.

(7) The Secretary of State may by order designate for the purpose of this section bodies appearing to him to be eligible in accordance with subsection (8) below and, with respect to any body designated by it, any such order—

(a) shall specify the classes of body to whom the designated body may grant permits ;

(b) may impose restrictions with respect to the grant of permits by the designated body and, in particular, may provide that no permit may be granted, either generally or in such cases as may be specified in the order, unless there are attached to the permit such conditions as may be so specified ; and

(c) may require the body to make returns with regard to the permits granted by it.

(8) A body is eligible in accordance with this subsection if it is concerned with—

(a) education ;

(b) religion ;

(c) social welfare ;

(d) recreation ; or

(e) other activities of benefit to the community.

(9) A body may hold more than one permit but may not use more than one bus at any one time under the same permit.

Further provision with respect to permits under section 19.

20.—(1) Subject to subsection (2) below, a permit shall specify the body to whom it is granted.

(2) A permit may be granted to a named individual on behalf of a body if, having regard to the nature of that body, it appears to the traffic commissioner or body granting the permit appropriate to do so.

(3) Where a permit is granted to a named individual on behalf of a body, it shall be treated for the purposes of this section and section 19 of this Act as granted to that body.

(4) In addition to any conditions attached to such a permit by virtue of section 19(7)(*b*) of this Act, the traffic commissioner or other body granting such a permit may attach to it such conditions as he or that body considers appropriate, including, in particular, conditions—

(*a*) limiting the passengers who may be carried in any bus used under the permit to persons falling within such classes as may be specified in the permit ; and

(*b*) with respect to such other matters as may be prescribed.

(5) Subject to subsection (6) below, a permit may be varied or revoked—

(*a*) by the traffic commissioner or body who granted it ; and

(*b*) in the case of a permit granted by a body designated under section 19(7) of this Act, after consultation with that body, by the traffic commissioner for any traffic area in which any bus has been used under the permit.

(6) A permit may not be varied so as to substitute another body for the body to whom it was granted.

(7) A permit shall remain in force until—

(*a*) it is revoked under subsection (5) above ; or

(*b*) in the case of a permit granted by a body designated under section 19(7) of this Act, that body ceases to be so designated.

21.—(1) Regulations may prescribe—

Permits under section 19: regulations.

(*a*) the conditions to be fulfilled by any person driving a bus while it is being used under a permit ;

(*b*) the conditions as to fitness which are to be fulfilled by any small bus used under a permit ;

(*c*) the form of permits ; and

(*d*) the documents, plates and marks to be carried by any bus while it is being used under a permit and the manner and position in which they are to be carried.

(2) Where regulations are made by virtue of subsection (1)(*b*) above, section 6 of the 1981 Act (certificate of initial fitness for public service vehicles) shall not apply in relation to any small bus subject to the regulations.

(3) Regulations under this section may contain such transitional provisions as the Secretary of State thinks fit.

22.—(1) In this section and section 23 of this Act—

Community bus permits.

" community bus service " means a local service provided—

(*a*) by a body concerned for the social and welfare needs of one or more communities ;

(b) without a view to profit, either on the part of that body or of anyone else ; and

(c) by means of a vehicle adapted to carry more than eight but not more than sixteen passengers ; and

" community bus permit " means a permit granted under this section in relation to the use of a public service vehicle—

(a) in providing a community bus service ; or

(b) in providing a community bus service and (other than in the course of a local service) carrying passengers for hire or reward where the carriage of those passengers will directly assist the provision of the community bus service by providing financial support for it.

(2) A community bus permit may be granted by the traffic commissioner for the area in which the operating centre for any vehicle used under the permit will be.

(3) A traffic commissioner shall not grant a community bus permit unless he is satisfied that there will be adequate facilities or arrangements for maintaining in a fit and serviceable condition any vehicle used under the permit.

(4) A body may hold more than one community bus permit but may not use more than one vehicle at any one time under the same permit.

Further provision with respect to community bus permits.

23.—(1) The requirements mentioned in subsection (2) below shall be conditions of every community bus permit and shall apply in relation to any use of a vehicle under such a permit.

(2) Those requirements are that—

(a) the driver receives no payment for driving except—

(i) reimbursement of any reasonable expenses incurred by him in making himself available to drive ; and

(ii) an amount representing any earnings lost as a result of making himself available to drive in exceptional circumstances ;

(b) the driver either holds a public service vehicle driver's licence or fulfils any conditions prescribed in relation to a person driving a vehicle which is being used under a community bus permit ; and

(c) any vehicle used under the permit fulfils any prescribed conditions of fitness for such use.

(3) A traffic commissioner may at any time attach to a community bus permit granted by him such conditions (or additional conditions) of a prescribed description as he thinks fit

for restricting or regulating the use of any vehicle under the permit.

(4) The traffic commissioner by whom a community bus permit was granted may at any time while the permit is in force vary or remove any condition attached to it under subsection (3) above.

(5) Subject to section 68(3) of the 1981 Act (as applied by section 127(4) of this Act), if a condition attached to a community bus permit is contravened, the holder of the permit shall be liable on summary conviction to a fine not exceeding level 3 on the standard scale.

(6) The traffic commissioner by whom a community bus permit was granted may at any time revoke the permit on the ground—

(a) that he is no longer satisfied with respect to the adequacy of facilities or arrangements for maintaining in a fit and serviceable condition any vehicle used under the permit ;

(b) that there has been a contravention of any condition attached to the permit ; or

(c) that a prohibition under section 9 of the 1981 Act (power to prohibit driving of unfit public service vehicles) has been imposed with respect to a vehicle used under the permit which has its operating centre in his area.

(7) Where regulations are made by virtue of subsection (2)(c) above, section 6 of the 1981 Act (certificate of initial fitness for public service vehicles) shall not apply in relation to any vehicle subject to the regulations.

(8) Regulations may prescribe—

(a) the form of community bus permits ; and

(b) the documents, plates and marks to be carried by any vehicle while it is being used under a community bus permit and the manner and position in which they are to be carried.

Further amendments with respect to PSV operators' licences

24.—(1) In section 16 of the 1981 Act (conditions attached to PSV operators' licences)—

Limit on number of vehicles to be used under a restricted licence.

(a) the following subsection shall be inserted after subsection (1)—

" (1A) In the case of a restricted licence, the number specified as the maximum in any condition imposed under subsection (1) above shall not, except in any prescribed case or class of case, exceed two." ;

B

(*b*) in subsection (8) of that section (power of traffic commissioner to dispense temporarily with conditions attached under that subsection), after the words " under this section " there shall be inserted the words " (other than a condition so attached under subsection (1A) above) " ; and

(*c*) in subsection (9) of that section (limited effect of conditions attached under subsection (1)), after the words " subsection (1) " there shall be inserted the words " or (1A) ".

(2) In section 18(2) of that Act (traffic commissioner to supply to holder of PSV operator's licence operators' discs for the number of vehicles authorised to be used under the licence)—

(*a*) after the words " section 16(1) " there shall be inserted the words " or (1A) " ;

(*b*) after the words " and if " there shall be inserted the words " (in the case of any condition or conditions attached under section 16(1)) ".

Objections to application for PSV operator's licence.

25. After section 14 of the 1981 Act (grant of licences) there shall be inserted the following section—

" Objections to application for PSV operator's licence.

14A.—(1) Where an application is made for the grant of a PSV operator's licence under this Act, any chief officer of police or local authority may object to the grant of the licence on the ground that one or more of the requirements mentioned in section 14(1) and (3) of this Act are not satisfied in relation to the application.

(2) An objection under this section shall be made within the prescribed time and in the prescribed manner and shall contain particulars of the ground on which it is made.

(3) The onus of proof of the existence of the ground on which an objection is made shall lie on the objector.

(4) In this section " local authority " means—

(*a*) in England and Wales, the council of a county, district or London borough or the Common Council of the City of London or a Passenger Transport Executive ; and

(*b*) in Scotland, a regional or islands council.

(5) This section does not apply in relation to any application for a special licence (within the meaning of section 12 of the Transport Act 1985)."

26.—(1) Where it appears to a traffic commissioner, in relation to a person ("the operator") to whom he has granted or
is proposing to grant a PSV operator's licence, that—

    (*a*) the operator has failed to operate a local service regis-
tered under section 6 of this Act ; or

    (*b*) the operator has operated a local service in contraven-
tion of that section ; or

    (*c*) the arrangements for maintaining the vehicles used
under the licence in a fit and serviceable condition are
not adequate for the use of those vehicles in providing
the local service or services in question ; or

    (*d*) the operator, or any employee or agent of his, has—

        (i) intentionally interfered with the operation of a
local service provided by another operator ;

        (ii) operated a local service in a manner dangerous
to the public ; or

        (iii) been guilty of any other serious misconduct
(whether or not constituting a criminal offence) in
relation to the operation of a local service ; or

    (*e*) a condition attached under section 8 of this Act to the
operator's licence has been contravened ;

he may (on granting the licence or at any later time) attach to
it either a condition prohibiting the operator from using vehicles
under the licence to provide any local service of a description
specified in the condition or one prohibiting him from so using
vehicles to provide local services of any description.

(2) The commissioner may attach a condition to a PSV
operator's licence under subsection (1) above, by reference to
circumstances falling within paragraph (*a*) or (*b*) of that subsection if, but only if, it appears to him that the operator did
not have a reasonable excuse for his conduct or that it is appropriate to attach the condition in view of—

    (*a*) the danger to the public involved in the operator's
conduct ; or

    (*b*) the frequency of conduct of the kind in question on
the part of the operator.

(3) Where the effect of a condition attached to a PSV
operator's licence under subsection (1) above is that the operator
of a local service registered under section 6 of this Act is prohibited from using vehicles under the licence to provide that
service, the traffic commissioner attaching the condition may—

    (*a*) cancel the registration ; or

    (*b*) where the service is registered with another traffic com-
missioner, direct that it be cancelled.

(4) Where a direction is given under subsection (3)(*b*) above, it shall be the duty of the traffic commissioner with whom the service is registered to cancel the registration.

(5) Where it appears to the commissioner that—

    (*a*) vehicles used under the licence (or under any PSV operator's licence previously held by the operator) have not been maintained in a fit and serviceable condition ; or

    (*b*) the operator has been involved in arrangements with any other operator for the use of each other's vehicles with a view to hindering enforcement of any requirements of the law relating to the operation of those vehicles ;

he may (on granting the licence or at any later time) attach to the licence a condition restricting the vehicles which the operator may use under the licence to vehicles specified in the condition.

(6) A condition attached to a licence under subsection (5) above shall—

    (*a*) apply only to vehicles which have their operating centre in the traffic area for which the commissioner acts ; and

    (*b*) be in addition to (and not be taken as prejudicing in any way) any conditions attached to the licence under section 16 of the 1981 Act as to the maximum number of vehicles which the operator may at any one time use under the licence.

27.—(1) Before attaching any condition to a PSV operator's licence under section 26 of this Act, a traffic commissioner shall hold an inquiry if he has, within the prescribed period, received a request for an inquiry from the holder of, or (as the case may be) applicant for, the licence.

(2) Subsection (1) above shall not apply where the traffic commissioner is satisfied that the condition should be attached without delay.

(3) Where, in reliance on subsection (2) above, a traffic commissioner attaches any such condition to a PSV operator's licence without first holding an inquiry, he shall hold one as soon as is reasonably practicable if the holder of the licence has, before the end of such period as may be prescribed, asked him to do so.

(4) For the purposes of section 16(5) of the 1981 Act (traffic commissioner's power to vary or remove conditions attached under section 16(3) of that Act to a PSV operator's licence), a condition attached under section 26 of this Act shall be treated as attached under section 16(3) of that Act.

(5) Nothing in section 26 shall be taken as prejudicing the generality of the power under that Act to prescribe descriptions of conditions for the purposes of section 16(3) of that Act.

28.—(1) Where the traffic commissioner for any traffic area revokes a PSV operator's licence, he may order the former holder to be disqualified, indefinitely or for such period as he thinks fit, from holding or obtaining a PSV operator's licence.

(2) So long as a disqualification imposed under subsection (1) above is in force with respect to any person, no PSV operator's licence shall be granted to him and any such licence obtained by him shall be of no effect.

(3) An order under subsection (1) above may be limited so as to apply only to the holding or obtaining of a PSV operator's licence in respect of the area of one or more specified traffic commissioners and, if the order is so limited, subsection (2) above shall apply only to any PSV operator's licence to which the order applies.

(4) Where a traffic commissioner makes an order under subsection (1) above with respect to any person, he may direct that if that person, at any time during such period as he may specify—

(a) is a director of, or holds a controlling interest in—

(i) a company which holds a licence of the kind to which the order applies ; or

(ii) a company of which a company which holds such a licence is a subsidiary ; or

(b) operates any public service vehicles in partnership with a person who holds such a licence ;

the powers under section 17(2) of the 1981 Act (revocation, suspension, etc., of PSV operators' licences) shall be exercisable in relation to that licence by the traffic commissioner by whom it was granted.

(5) The powers conferred by this section in relation to the person who was the holder of a licence shall be exercisable also—

(a) where that person was a company, in relation to any officer of that company ; and

(b) where that person operated the vehicles used under the licence in partnership with other persons, in relation to any of those other persons.

(6) A traffic commissioner shall not make any such order or give any such direction without first holding an inquiry if any person affected by the proposed order or direction requests him to do so.

(7) For the purposes of this section a person holds a controlling interest in a company if he is the beneficial owner of more than half its equity share capital.

PART I
Duty to give
Secretary of
State
information
about certain
matters.

29. In subsections (1) and (2) of section 20 of the 1981 Act (which require the holder of a PSV operator's licence to inform the traffic commissioners of certain kinds of failure of, or damage or alteration to, a public service vehicle owned by him), for the words " traffic commissioners who granted the licence " there shall be substituted the words " Secretary of State ".

Plying for
hire by large
public service
vehicles.

30.—(1) A public service vehicle which is adapted to carry more than eight passengers shall not be used on a road in plying for hire as a whole.

(2) Subject to section 68(3) of the 1981 Act (as applied by section 127(4) of this Act), if a vehicle is used in contravention of subsection (1) above, the operator of the vehicle shall be liable on summary conviction to a fine not exceeding level 3 on the standard scale.

Appeals
under the
1981 Act.

31. For sections 50 and 51 of the 1981 Act (appeals) there shall be substituted the following sections—

"Appeals to
the
Transport
Tribunal.

50.—(1) An applicant for the grant of a PSV operator's licence under this Act may appeal to the Transport Tribunal against any decision of the traffic commissioner—

> (a) to refuse to grant the licence in accordance with the application ; or
>
> (b) to attach any condition to the licence otherwise than in accordance with the application.

(2) Where a person who has applied for a new PSV operator's licence in substitution for a licence held by him and in force at the date of his application appeals to the Transport Tribunal under subsection (1) above, the existing licence shall continue in force until the appeal is disposed of, but without prejudice to the exercise in the meantime of the powers conferred by section 17 of this Act.

(3) Where an application for a PSV operator's licence is granted under this Act and a person who duly made an objection to the grant under section 14A of this Act is aggrieved by the grant of the licence he may appeal to the Transport Tribunal.

(4) The holder of a PSV operator's licence may appeal to the Transport Tribunal against any decision of the traffic commissioner—

> (a) to refuse his application for the variation or removal of any condition attached to the licence ;

(*b*) to vary any such condition, or to attach any new condition to the licence, otherwise than on his application ; or

(*c*) to revoke or suspend the licence or to curtail its period of validity.

(5) Where—

(*a*) the holder of a PSV operator's licence in respect of which an order or direction has been made or given under section 28 of the Transport Act 1985 (power to disqualify PSV operators) ; or

(*b*) any person in respect of whom any such order or direction has been made or given ;

is aggrieved by the order or direction he may appeal to the Transport Tribunal.

(6) The traffic commissioner—

(*a*) making any such decision with respect to a licence as is mentioned in subsection (4)(*b*) or (*c*) above ;

(*b*) making any such order or giving any such direction as is mentioned in subsection (5) above ;

may, if the holder of the licence or any such person as is mentioned in subsection (5)(*b*) above so requests, direct that his decision shall not have effect until the expiration of the period within which an appeal against it may be made to the Transport Tribunal and, if an appeal is made, until it is disposed of.

(7) Where a traffic commissioner has given a direction under subsection (6) above he may withdraw it at any time.

(8) If the traffic commissioner refuses to give a direction under subsection (6) above or withdraws such a direction, the person requesting it may apply for such a direction to the Transport Tribunal and the Transport Tribunal shall give their decision on the application within fourteen days.

(9) This section does not apply in relation to conditions attached to a PSV operator's licence under section 8 of the Transport Act 1985 (enforcement of traffic regulation conditions).

Appeals to the Secretary of State.

51.—(1) A person applying for—

(*a*) a certificate of initial fitness under section 6 of this Act ; or (*b*) a certificate under section 10 of this Act that a vehicle conforms to a type vehicle;

may appeal to the Secretary of State against the refusal of a certifying officer to issue such a certificate.

(2) Where the refusal by a certifying officer or public service vehicle examiner to remove a prohibition under subsection (1) of section 9 of this Act (including a prohibition under that subsection as it applies by virtue of section 9A of this Act) has been referred to a certifying officer (" the referee ") under subsection (8) of that section by a traffic commissioner, any person aggrieved by the refusal of the referee to remove the prohibition may appeal to the Secretary of State.

(3) An appeal under this section must be made within the prescribed time and in the prescribed manner; and provision may be made by regulations as to the procedure to be followed in connection with such appeals.

(4) On the determination of an appeal under this section, the Secretary of State may confirm, vary or reverse the decision appealed against, and may give such directions as he thinks fit to the certifying officer for giving effect to his decision; and it shall be the duty of the certifying officer to comply with any such directions."

Miscellaneous

Repeal of sections 28, 47 and 48 of the 1981 Act.

32. The following provisions of the 1981 Act shall cease to have effect—

(*a*) section 28 (terms and conditions of employment of persons employed by holders of PSV operators' licences); and

(*b*) sections 47 and 48 (experimental areas).

Extension of safety controls to certain passenger vehicles other than public service vehicles.

33. The following section shall be inserted in the 1981 Act after section 9 (prohibition on driving unfit public service vehicle following inspection under section 8)—

" Extension of sections 8 and 9 to certain passenger vehicles other than public service vehicles.

9A.—(1) Section 8 of this Act shall apply, with the omission of subsection (1)(*b*), to any motor vehicle (other than a tramcar) which is adapted to carry more than eight passengers but is not a public service vehicle as it applies to a public service vehicle.

(2) Section 9 of this Act shall apply to any such motor vehicle as it applies to a public service vehicle with the omission of subsection (4)."

PART II

REGULATION OF ROAD PASSENGER TRANSPORT IN LONDON

London local service licences

34.—(1) In this Act " London local service " means (subject London local to subsection (3) below) a local service with one or more stopping services. places in London.

(2) In this Part of this Act—

(a) " bus service " means a local service other than an excursion or tour ; and

(b) " London bus service " means a London local service other than an excursion or tour.

(3) Where a local service is or is to be provided both inside and outside London, any part of the service which is or is to be provided outside London shall be treated as a separate service for the purposes of this Act if there is any stopping place for that part of the service outside London.

35.—(1) Subject to subsection (2) below and to section 36 of London local this Act, a London local service shall not be provided except service under a London local service licence granted in accordance with licences. the following provisions of this Part of this Act.

(2) A London local service licence is not required for the provision by any person under an agreement with the Railways Board of any service secured by the Board under section 4A of the 1962 Act (Board's power to secure the provision of bus services where a railway service has been temporarily interrupted or discontinued).

(3) The traffic commissioner for the Metropolitan Traffic Area (referred to below in this Part of this Act as the metropolitan traffic commissioner) shall be responsible for granting London local service licences.

(4) Subject to subsection (5) below and to section 39(4) of this Act, a London local service licence shall be of no effect at any time at which the holder does not also hold—

(a) a PSV operator's licence granted by the metropolitan traffic commissioner or by the traffic commissioner for any other traffic area, not being a licence which is at that time of no effect by reason of its suspension ; or

(b) a permit under section 22 of this Act.

(5) Subsection (4) above does not apply to a London local service licence held by a local education authority.

(6) Subject to section 68(3) of the 1981 Act (as applied by section 127(4) of this Act), if a London local service is provided in contravention of subsection (1) above, the operator of the service shall be liable on summary conviction to a fine not exceeding level 3 on the standard scale.

London bus
services under
control of
London
Regional
Transport.

1984 c. 32.

36.—(1) A London local service licence is not required for the provision of a London bus service—

    (a) by London Regional Transport or any subsidiary of theirs ; or

    (b) by any other person in pursuance of any agreement entered into by London Regional Transport by virtue of section 3(2) of the London Regional Transport Act 1984 (referred to below in this section as the 1984 Act).

(2) Where—

    (a) London Regional Transport or any subsidiary of theirs propose to provide a new bus service which is to be operated wholly or in part as a London bus service or to vary a bus service currently provided by them which is being so operated ; or

    (b) London Regional Transport propose to enter into an agreement by virtue of section 3(2) of the 1984 Act for the provision of such a new bus service by any other person or to agree to a variation in any bus service currently provided in pursuance of any such agreement which is being so operated ;

then, before deciding on, or on the provisions to be contained in any such agreement with respect to, or on any variation affecting, any relevant aspects of that service London Regional Transport shall, so far as the service is or is to be provided in London, consult with the commissioner or commissioners of police concerned, with the local authorities affected, with the Passengers' Committee and with any other person they think fit.

(3) In subsection (2) above the reference to relevant aspects of the service is a reference to the route of the service, a terminal point, a point at which passengers may or may not be taken up or set down, or a place at which, or street by the use of which, vehicles used for the service may turn at a terminal point.

(4) Where—

    (a) London Regional Transport or any subsidiary of theirs propose to discontinue a bus service currently provided by them which is being operated wholly or in part as a London bus service ; or (*b*) London Regional Transport propose not to renew any agreement entered into by them by virtue of section 3(2) of the 1984 Act for the provision by any other person of any bus service which is being so operated, or to agree to the discontinuance of any such bus service currently provided in pursuance of any such agreement ;

then, before any decision is taken to that effect, London Regional Transport shall, so far as the service is provided in London, consult with the local authorities affected, with the Passengers' Committee and with any other person they think fit.

(5) Where an agreement entered into by London Regional Transport by virtue of section 3(2) of the 1984 Act for the provision of a bus service relates to such a service part only of which is operated as a London bus service, any provision contained in that agreement with respect to the carriage of passengers other than those who are both taken up and set down in London shall be of no effect if or so far as it is inconsistent with any condition for the time being attached under section 8 of this Act to—

(*a*) a PSV operator's licence ; or

(*b*) a permit under section 22 of this Act ;

held by the operator of the service.

(6) For the purposes of this section the local authorities affected by any proposal with respect to a bus service are any of the following councils, that is to say, the councils of the London boroughs and the Common Council, in whose area there is situated—

(*a*) in the case of a proposal to which subsection (2) above applies, any part of the route in question or (as the case may be) the point, place or street in question ; or

(*b*) in the case of a proposal to which subsection (4) above applies, any part of the route of the service.

(7) In this section—

(*a*) references to a new bus service are references to a bus service which has not been provided continuously since before the date on which this section comes into force (disregarding, in the case of a bus service operated during certain periods of the year only, any period other than one during which the service is due to be operated) ;

(*b*) " the Passengers' Committee " means the London Regional Passengers' Committee established under section 40 of the 1984 Act ;

(c) " subsidiary " has the same meaning as in that Act ;

and section 6(5) of and paragraph 11(4) of Schedule 5 to that Act shall apply to references in this section to an agreement entered into by London Regional Transport by virtue of section 3(2) of that Act as they apply to such references in that Act.

37.—(1) An application for a London local service licence shall be made in such a form as the metropolitan traffic commissioner may require, and an applicant shall give the commissioner such information as he may reasonably require for disposing of the application.

(2) Where an application is made for the grant of a London local service licence, the commissioner—

(a) shall grant the licence unless he is satisfied that to do so would be against the interests of the public ; and

(b) if he grants the licence, shall do so in accordance with the application except to the extent that he is satisfied that to do so would be against the interests of the public.

(3) In considering under subsection (2) above whether the grant of a licence would be against the interests of the public, or the extent to which the grant of a licence in accordance with the application would be against those interests, the commissioner shall in particular have regard to—

(a) the transport needs for the time being of London as a whole and of particular communities within London ;

(b) any transport policies or plans which have been made and drawn to his attention by the council of a London borough or by the Common Council ; and

(c) any objections or other representations made to the commissioner in the prescribed manner which in his opinion are relevant.

(4) The metropolitan traffic commissioner, on granting a London local service licence, shall send notice of the grant, including particulars of the services to be provided under the licence, to the commissioner or commissioners of police concerned and to each of the local authorities affected.

38.—(1) Subject to subsection (3) below, and to any regulations, the metropolitan traffic commissioner may, on granting a London local service licence, attach to the licence such conditions as he thinks fit having regard to the interests of the public, and in particular to the matters mentioned in section 37(3)(a) to (c) of this Act.

(2) The conditions that may be attached to a London local service licence by virtue of subsection (1) above include, in par-

ticular, such conditions as the commissioner thinks fit for securing—

> (a) that suitable routes are used in providing any service which may be provided under the licence ; and
>
> (b) that passengers are not taken up or are not set down except at specified points, or are not taken up or are not set down between specified points ;

and generally for securing the safety and convenience of the public, including persons who are elderly or disabled.

(3) No condition as to fares shall be attached under this section to a London local service licence.

(4) The metropolitan traffic commissioner may at any time while a London local service licence is in force vary the licence by—

> (a) altering, in such manner as he thinks fit having regard to the interests of the public, any condition attached to the licence ; or
>
> (b) removing any condition attached to the licence, if he thinks fit having regard to those interests ; or
>
> (c) attaching to the licence any such condition or additional condition as he thinks fit having regard to those interests.

(5) Where the holder of such a licence makes an application to the commissioner requesting him to exercise his powers under subsection (4) above, the commissioner shall exercise those powers in accordance with the application except to the extent that he is satisfied that to do so would be against the interests of the public.

(6) Compliance with any condition attached to a London local service licence under this section may be temporarily dispensed with by the commissioner if he is satisfied—

> (a) that compliance with the condition would be unduly onerous by reason of circumstances not foreseen when the condition was attached or, if the condition has been altered, when it was last altered ; and
>
> (b) that such a dispensation would not be against the interests of the public.

(7) Subject to section 68(3) of the 1981 Act (as applied by section 127(4) of this Act), if a condition attached under this section to a London local service licence is contravened, the holder of the licence shall be liable on summary conviction to a fine not exceeding level 3 on the standard scale.

Part II
Grant of
licences for
certain
excursions or
tours.

39.—(1) This section applies where, in the case of any application for a London local service licence, the metropolitan traffic commissioner is satisfied that the service which the applicant proposes to provide under the licence (" the proposed service ") would be an excursion or tour and is also satisfied either—

(a) that the proposed service would not compete directly with any authorised London bus service ; or

(b) that the proposed service would operate only to enable passengers to attend special events.

(2) In subsection (1)(a) above, " authorised London bus service " means—

(a) any London bus service for which a London local service licence has been granted ; and

(b) any London bus service which, by virtue of section 36(1) of this Act, does not require a London local service licence.

(3) In any case to which this section applies, sections 35, 37 and 38 of this Act shall apply subject to the modifications provided by the following provisions of this section.

(4) Section 35(4) of this Act shall not prevent a London local service licence granted in pursuance of this section from having effect for the purposes of the provision of a service by means of a vehicle whose operator holds any such licence or permit as is there mentioned (not being, in the case of a PSV operator's licence, a licence which is for the time being of no effect by reason of its suspension).

(5) The interests of the public falling to be considered under any provision of section 37 or 38 shall be confined to the interests of the public in securing that only places which are suitable for use as such are used as stopping places for the service in question in London.

The reference above in this subsection to the service in question is a reference to the proposed service or the service provided under any London local service licence granted on an application to which this section applies (as the case may require).

(6) For the purposes of this section a place is to be regarded as not being suitable for use as a stopping place for any service if the commissioner is satisfied that its use as such would be prejudicial to the safety or convenience of the public.

(7) Section 37 shall apply with the omission of paragraphs (a) and (b) of subsection (3) ; and paragraph (c) of that subsection shall apply only in relation to objections or representations made by the commissioner or commissioners of police concerned or by any of the local authorities affected.

(8) Section 38 shall apply with the omission of subsections (1) and (2), but the metropolitan traffic commissioner in granting a licence on any application to which this section applies may attach to the licence such conditions of a description within section 38(2)(*b*) as he thinks fit, having regard to any objections or other representations that fall to be considered in relation to that application by virtue of section 37(3)(*c*), for securing that only places which are suitable for use as such are used as stopping places for the proposed service in London.

(9) Any condition attached to a licence under subsection (8) above shall be treated for the purposes of section 38(6) and (7) as if it had been attached under that section.

(10) Every London local service licence granted in pursuance of this section shall include a statement that it is so granted.

40.—(1) Subject to subsection (2) below, a London local service licence may be revoked or suspended by the metropolitan traffic commissioner on the ground that there has been a contravention of any condition attached to it.

(2) The commissioner shall not revoke or suspend a London local service licence unless, owing to the frequency of the breach of conditions, or to the breach having been committed intentionally, or to the danger to the public involved in the breach, the commissioner is satisfied that the licence should be revoked or suspended.

(3) On revoking or suspending a London local service licence the metropolitan traffic commissioner shall send notice of the revocation or suspension to every commissioner of police or local authority notified of the grant of the licence in accordance with section 37(4) of this Act.

(4) A London local service licence suspended under this section shall during the time of suspension be of no effect.

41.—(1) Subject to subsection (2) below, a London local service licence shall, unless previously revoked, continue in force until the end of the period of five years beginning with the date on which it takes effect, unless at the time of the granting of the licence the metropolitan traffic commissioner for special reasons determines that it shall continue in force only for a shorter period, in which case it shall, unless previously revoked, continue in force only until the end of that shorter period.

(2) If, on the date on which a London local service licence is due to expire, proceedings are pending before the metropolitan traffic commissioner on an application for the grant of a new licence in substitution for it, the existing licence shall continue

in force until the application is disposed of, but without prejudice to the exercise in the meantime of the powers conferred by section 40 of this Act.

(3) Nothing in this section shall prevent—

> (a) the grant of a London local service licence limited to one or more particular periods or occasions; or
>
> (b) the attachment to a London local service licence of a condition that the service shall be so limited.

Supplementary provisions

Appeals to
the Secretary
of State.

42.—(1) A person who has applied for the grant of a London local service licence may appeal to the Secretary of State against any decision of the metropolitan traffic commissioner—

> (a) to refuse to grant the licence in accordance with the application; or
>
> (b) to attach any condition to the licence otherwise than in accordance with the application.

(2) Where a person who has applied for a new London local service licence in substitution for a licence held by him and in force at the date of his application appeals to the Secretary of State under subsection (1) above against any such decision as is mentioned in paragraph (a) or (b) of that subsection, the existing licence shall continue in force until the appeal is disposed of, but without prejudice to the exercise in the meantime of the powers conferred by section 40 of this Act.

(3) The holder of a London local service licence may appeal to the Secretary of State against any decision of the metropolitan traffic commissioner—

> (a) to refuse an application by the holder for the variation or removal of any condition attached to the licence;
>
> (b) to vary any such condition, or to attach any new condition to the licence, otherwise than on an application by the holder; or
>
> (c) to revoke or suspend the licence.

(4) Where the commissioner makes any such decision with respect to a licence as is mentioned in subsection (3)(b) or (c) above he may, if the holder of the licence so requests, direct that his decision shall not have effect until the expiration of the period within which an appeal against it may be made to the Secretary of State under that subsection and, if such an appeal is made, until the appeal is disposed of.

(5) If the commissioner refuses to give a direction under subsection (4) above, the holder of the licence may apply to the

Secretary of State for such a direction, and the Secretary of State shall give his decision on the application within fourteen days.

(6) A person who has applied for the grant of a London local service licence, or for the variation or removal of any conditions attached to such a licence, shall, if the metropolitan traffic commissioner fails to come to a decision on the application within a reasonable time, have the same right to appeal to the Secretary of State as if the commissioner had decided to refuse the application.

(7) A person other than the applicant for, or holder of, a London local service licence may, if he has standing in the matter in accordance with the following provisions of this section, appeal to the Secretary of State against any decision of the metropolitan traffic commissioner with respect to—

(a) the grant, revocation or suspension of a London local service licence ; or

(h) the attachment of any condition to a London local service licence or the variation or removal of any condition attached to such a licence.

(8) Subject to subsection (9) below, the persons having standing to appeal under subsection (7) above against a decision of the metropolitan traffic commissioner with respect to a London local service licence are—

(a) any local authority affected ; and

(b) any person providing transport facilities along or near the route, or part of the route, of the service which is being or is to be provided under the licence ;

being a local authority or person who has made objections or other representations to the commissioner in the course of the proceedings resulting in that decision.

(9) Subsection (8)(b) above shall not apply in the case of any decision of the metropolitan traffic commissioner on an application to which section 39 of this Act applies or with respect to a London local service licence granted in pursuance of that section.

(10) An appeal under this section must be made within the prescribed time and in the prescribed manner ; and provision may be made by regulations as to the procedure to be followed in connection with appeals under this section.

(11) On any appeal under this section the Secretary of State may, if he thinks fit, remit the matter to the metropolitan traffic commissioner for rehearing and determination by him ; and, if he does so, he may give to the commissioner such directions as he thinks fit with respect to the consideration to be given to any circumstances of the case.

(12) On the determination of an appeal under this section the Secretary of State may confirm, vary or reverse the decision appealed against, and may give such directions as he thinks fit to the metropolitan traffic commissioner for giving effect to his decision.

Further
appeals on
points of law.

43.—(1) An appeal lies to the High Court at the instance of any of the persons mentioned in subsection (2) below on any point of law arising from a decision of the Secretary of State on an appeal from a decision of the metropolitan traffic commissioner.

(2) The persons who may appeal against any such decision of the Secretary of State are—

(a) the person who appealed to the Secretary of State ;

(b) any person who had a right to appeal to the Secretary of State against the relevant decision of the commissioner but did not exercise that right ;

(c) any person who would have had a right of appeal to the Secretary of State against the relevant decision of the commissioner if aggrieved by that decision and who is aggrieved by the decision of the Secretary of State on the appeal ; and

(d) the metropolitan traffic commissioner.

(3) If on an appeal under this section the High Court is of opinion that the decision appealed against was erroneous in point of law, it shall remit the matter to the Secretary of State with the opinion of the court for rehearing and determination by him.

(4) No appeal to the Court of Appeal may be brought from a decision of the High Court under this section except with the leave of the High Court or the Court of Appeal.

Application
of provisions
of the 1981
Act.

44.—(1) The provisions of the 1981 Act mentioned in subsection (2) below shall apply in relation to the grant of London local service licences, or to London local service licences granted, under this Part of this Act, as they apply in relation to the grant of PSV operators' licences, or to PSV operators' licences granted, under that Act.

(2) Those provisions are—

section 57 (death, bankruptcy, etc., of licence holder) ;

section 58(2) (grant of licences to unincorporated body or to persons jointly) ; and

section 59 (regulations with respect to procedure on applications for licences).

(3) Section 84 of that Act (which relates to the effect of that Act in relation to general public interests) shall have effect as if the provisions of this Part of this Act were contained in that Act.

45.—(1) In this Part of this Act—
  " commissioner of police " means—

> (*a*) in relation to the metropolitan police district, the Commissioner of Police of the Metropolis ; and

> (*b*) in relation to the City of London, the Commissioner of Police for the City of London ;

  " the Common Council " means the Common Council of the City of London ;

  " bus service " and " London bus service " have the meanings given by section 34(2) of this Act ; and

  " metropolitan traffic commissioner " shall be read in accordance with section 35(3) of this Act.

(2) Subject to subsection (3) below, for the purposes of—

> (*a*) section 37(4) of this Act ; and

> (*b*) section 42(8)(*a*) of this Act ;

the local authorities affected are any of the following councils, that is to say, the councils of the London boroughs and the Common Council, in whose area the service, or any part of the service, is being or (as the case may be) is to be provided under the licence in question.

(3) For the purposes of—

> (*a*) section 39(7) of this Act ; and

> (*b*) section 42(8)(*a*) of this Act as it applies in a case within subsection (9) of that section ;

the local authorities affected are any of the councils mentioned in subsection (2) above in whose area there is situated any stopping place for the proposed service or (as the case may be) for the service which is being provided under the licence in question.

Repeal of Part II

46.—(1) The Secretary of State may by order repeal this Part of this Act.

(2) Any order made under this section may contain such supplementary, incidental, consequential and transitional provisions as may appear to the Secretary of State to be necessary or expedient (including provision making such amendments or repeals in any provision of this or any other Act as may appear

to the Secretary of State to be required in consequence of the repeal of this Part of this Act).

(3) No order shall be made under this section unless a draft of the order has been laid before, and approved by a resolution of, each House of Parliament.

PART III

THE NATIONAL BUS COMPANY

The Bus Company's disposal programme

Transfer of operations of the Bus Company to the private sector.

47.—(1) The National Bus Company (referred to below in this Part of this Act as the Bus Company) shall submit to the Secretary of State written proposals providing for—

(a) the disposal, in preparation for the dissolution of the Company, of the whole of their undertaking, with such exceptions only as may be specified in or determined in accordance with the proposals ;

(b) the disposal of the whole or any part of the undertaking, or of any particular property, rights or liabilities, of any of their subsidiaries the disposal of which appears to the Company to be appropriate in preparation for the dissolution of the Company ; and

(c) the arrangements to be made in preparation for the dissolution of the Company for any matter for which provision appears to the Company to be appropriate for the purposes of or in connection with the dissolution.

(2) Without prejudice to the generality of subsection (1)(c) above, the arrangements there mentioned may include provision for the making by the Company or any subsidiary of theirs, to persons employed by them or any such subsidiary who do not by virtue of any disposal in pursuance of the proposals fall to be treated as employed by any other person, of payments by way of compensation in respect of the loss of their employment.

(3) The proposals shall be submitted before the end of the period of three months beginning with the day on which this section comes into force or such further period as the Secretary of State may from time to time allow by notice in writing to the Company.

(4) In this Part of this Act " the Company's disposal programme " means (as the case may require)—

(a) the proposals submitted by the Company under this section ;

(b) those proposals as approved by the Secretary of State under subsection (7) below; or

(c) the proposals formulated by the Secretary of State under subsection (8) below;

(subject, in a case within paragraph (b) or (c) above, to any modifications under subsection (10) below).

(5) The Company's disposal programme shall describe—

(a) the general approach the Company plan to adopt in relation to the manner in which disposals for which the programme provides are to be carried out (including the intended time-scale for major stages in implementing the programme);

(b) the general scope and purpose of such disposals and the estimated effect at each such stage of the disposals carried out up to that time on any remaining operations of the Company and any of their subsidiaries;

(c) the measures (if any) which the Company propose to take, for the purpose of preparing for any such disposals, by way of reorganisation of the structure or operations of the Company and any of their subsidiaries; and

(d) the manner in which the Company's main objective under section 48(1) of this Act and their duties under subsections (3) and (4) of that section are to be implemented in relation to the proposals included in the programme.

(6) Without prejudice to the generality of subsection (5)(c) above, the measures there mentioned may include the formation or promotion of new subsidiaries and the reconstruction, amalgamation, dissolution or winding up of any existing subsidiaries.

(7) The Secretary of State may approve the Company's disposal programme without modifications or with such modifications as, after consultation with the Company, he thinks fit.

(8) If any proposals submitted by the Company under this section appear to the Secretary of State to be so defective, with respect to any matters those proposals are required in accordance with subsection (5) above to describe, as to be unsuitable for adopting (with any appropriate modifications) as a basis for carrying out the disposals mentioned in subsection (1) above the Secretary of State may, after consultation with the Company, formulate proposals of his own to have effect as the Company's disposal programme in substitution for the Company's proposals.

(9) When the Secretary of State has approved the Company's disposal programme or formulated proposals of his own to have

effect as that programme, it shall be the duty of the Company to implement the programme before the end of the period of three years beginning with the day on which this section comes into force or before such date after the end of that period as may be prescribed.

(10) The Secretary of State may from time to time, at the request of the Company or of his own motion, make such modifications in the Company's disposal programme as, after consultation with the Company, he thinks fit.

(11) The exercise by the Secretary of State of any of his powers under the preceding provisions of this section requires the consent of the Treasury.

(12) The Secretary of State may by order dissolve any company which is a subsidiary of the Bus Company and incorporated by local Act or by an order under the Light Railways Act 1896.

1896 c. 48.

(13) An order made under subsection (12) above may provide for the disposal of any remaining property, rights or liabilities of the company dissolved and may contain such supplementary, incidental and consequential provisions (including the repeal of any statutory provision) as appear to the Secretary of State to be necessary or expedient.

General duties of the Bus Company.

48.—(1) The main objective of the Bus Company—

    (*a*) in preparing their disposal programme ; and

    (*b*) in the conduct of their undertaking and the businesses of their subsidiaries after section 47 of this Act comes into force until the completion of that programme ;

shall be to promote sustained and fair competition, both between companies which are Bus group or former Bus group companies and between any such companies and other persons engaged in providing bus services or in carrying on any activities carried on in connection with providing bus services.

(2) For the purposes of subsection (1) above, Bus group companies are the Bus Company, their subsidiaries and any companies as respects which the Bus Company have any interest in their issued ordinary share capital.

(3) The Bus Company shall have regard—

    (*a*) in preparing their disposal programme ;

    (*b*) in taking any decisions in carrying out their programme with respect to disposals required in pursuance of the programme ; and

    (*c*) in the conduct of their undertaking and the businesses of their subsidiaries as mentioned in subsection (1)(*b*) above ;

to the estimated effect of any proposal, decision or other course of action under consideration on the net value that may be expected to be secured from all disposals so required.

That value is the excess of the aggregate proceeds arising from all disposals so required over the aggregate costs incurred in carrying out the programme and taking any other steps required in preparation for the dissolution of the Company.

(4) In carrying out their disposal programme, the Bus Company shall take such steps as may be practicable to secure that persons employed in any undertaking or part of an undertaking which is to be the subject of a disposal under the programme are afforded what appears to the Company to be a reasonable opportunity of acquiring (whether alone or jointly with other persons) a controlling interest in the equity share capital of any company operating or proposing to operate that undertaking or part.

(5) The Secretary of State may give directions to the Bus Company as to the manner in which they are to carry out their main objective under subsection (1) above, or their duty under subsection (3) or (4) above, in any respect or in any case specified in the directions; and a copy of any directions given by the Secretary of State under this section shall be laid before each House of Parliament.

Powers of disposal

49.—(1) Without prejudice to any powers conferred on them by any other enactment, the Bus Company shall have power to provide for the implementation, in such manner as they think fit, of any disposal required in pursuance of their disposal programme.

The Bus Company's powers of disposal.

(2) The Bus Company shall not exercise their powers under subsection (1) above in relation to any disposal so required except with the consent of the Secretary of State; but that consent may be given either—

    (*a*) generally, in relation to disposals of any specified description; or

    (*b*) in relation to a particular disposal.

(3) In providing in exercise of their powers under subsection (1) above for the disposal of any shares in or other securities of any subsidiary of theirs, the Bus Company may, with the consent of the Secretary of State, provide for employees' share schemes to be established in respect of that subsidiary; and any such scheme may provide for the transfer of shares without consideration.

50.—(1) For the purpose of facilitating the eventual implementation of any disposal required in pursuance of their disposal programme, the Bus Company may exercise their powers to form subsidiaries and to transfer property, rights and liabilities to subsidiaries, notwithstanding the provisions of any enactment which may be taken to limit the purposes for which those powers may be exercised.

(2) The Bus Company may also, for that purpose, make schemes for the transfer of any property, rights or liabilities between the Company and a wholly-owned subsidiary of theirs or between one such subsidiary and another.

(3) A scheme under subsection (2) above shall not come into force until it has been approved by the Secretary of State or until such date as the Secretary of State may, in giving his approval, specify ; and the Secretary of State may approve a scheme either without modifications or with such modifications as, after consultation with the Bus Company, he thinks fit.

(4) On the coming into force of a scheme under subsection (2) above the property, rights and liabilities affected by the scheme shall, subject to section 129 of this Act, be transferred and vest in accordance with the scheme.

51.—(1) Subject to subsection (2) below, the Bus Company may provide for any related company any of the services which they have power to provide for any of their subsidiaries.

(2) The Bus Company shall make proper commercial charges for any services provided under this section.

(3) In this section and section 52 of this Act " related company " means a company as respects which the Bus Company have, or at any time have had, an interest in not less than twenty per cent. of its issued ordinary share capital.

52.—(1) The Secretary of State may make such orders under section 74 of the 1962 Act (power to make provision about pensions in the nationalised transport industry) in relation to related companies as he could make if those companies were subsidiaries of the Bus Company.

(2) In exercising with respect to any pension scheme the powers conferred by this section, the Secretary of State shall take into account any representations made by the persons administering the scheme.

(3) Except on the application of a related company which is not a subsidiary of the Bus Company, no order shall be made by virtue of this section which has the effect of placing the

related company or any of its subsidiaries in any worse position ; but for the purposes of this subsection a related company or a subsidiary shall not be regarded as being placed in a worse position because an order provides that any changes in a pension scheme are not to be effected without the consent of the Secretary of State.

(4) Any order such as is mentioned in subsection (3) above which is made otherwise than on the application of the related company shall not be invalid because it does not have the effect of securing that the related company and its subsidiaries are not placed in any worse position, but except in so far as the related company approves the effect of the order the Secretary of State shall as soon as may be make the necessary amending order.

(5) Subsections (3) and (4) above have effect only in relation to orders made after such day as may be appointed for the purposes of this section by order made by the Secretary of State, and different days may be so appointed in relation to different related companies.

(6) Where an order (the " first order ") applying to a related company has been made under section 74 and at the time when it was made the related company was a subsidiary of the Bus Company, the order shall not apply to the related company when it ceases to be such a subsidiary except where an order made (at any time) by virtue of this section provides for the first order to continue to apply to the related company.

(7) An order made by virtue of this section may, in particular, authorise the Bus Company or any subsidiary of the Company—

(a) to transfer liabilities under a pension scheme in relation to some (but not all) of the participants in that scheme to another pension scheme ; and

(b) to divide or apportion a pension fund held for the purposes of the first-mentioned scheme between that scheme and the other scheme.

(8) In this section " participant ", in relation to a scheme, means—

(a) in relation to a scheme under which benefits are or will be receivable as of right, a person who has pension rights under the scheme (whether he has contributed or not) ; and

(b) in relation to a scheme under which benefits are not or will not be receivable as of right, a person who (whether he is referred to in the scheme as a member, contributor or otherwise) has contributed under the scheme and has pension rights under it.

Miscellaneous and supplementary

53.—(1) The Secretary of State may from time to time by order extinguish the liability of the Bus Company in respect of the principal of, and any outstanding interest on, all or any sums lent to the Company by the Secretary of State under section 20 of the 1962 Act.

(2) The Secretary of State may from time to time give directions to the Company requiring the Company to make to him, out of the net proceeds of any disposals made in pursuance of the Company's disposal programme, payments of such amounts, at such times and by such methods, as may be specified in the directions.

(3) Such payments shall, if and to the extent that the Secretary of State so directs, be applied in repayment of any sums lent to the Company as mentioned in subsection (1) above or in payment of any interest outstanding on any such sums.

(4) Sums received under subsection (2) above which are applied as mentioned in subsection (3) above shall be treated—

(a) for the purposes of section 20(5) of the 1962 Act as received under section 20(2) ; and

(b) for the purposes of section 44(1) of the 1968 Act (account by Secretary of State of receipt and disposal of certain sums) as received by way of interest on, or the repayment of, a loan to the Company under section 20(1).

(5) Sums received under subsection (2) above which are not so applied shall be paid into the Consolidated Fund.

(6) Any agreement or arrangements entered into by the Company or any subsidiary of theirs in connection with any disposal made in pursuance of the disposal programme may, with the approval of the Secretary of State, include provision—

(a) for the maintenance to any extent of any concession, benefit or privilege enjoyed by—

(i) any person who is or has been employed by the Company (or any subsidiary of theirs) ; or

(ii) a member of such a person's family ; or

(b) for the making of any payment or the provision of any other concession, benefit or privilege in compensation for the loss, reduction or limitation of that concession, benefit or privilege ;

and the Company may make payments to any person in pursuance of or for the purpose of securing any such provision.

(7) Without prejudice to the generality of section 47(1)(c) of this Act, the arrangements there mentioned may include provision for the making by the Company of payments in com-

pensation for any loss, reduction or limitation of any such concession, benefit or privilege as is mentioned in subsection (6) above to the extent that provision in respect of the loss, reduction or limitation is not made by virtue of that subsection.

(8) The power of the Secretary of State to make an order under subsection (1) above shall be subject to the approval of the Treasury and any such order shall be subject to annulment in pursuance of a resolution of the Commons House of Parliament.

54.—(1) When it appears to the Secretary of State that the Bus Company have completed their disposal programme, the Secretary of State may by order provide for the dissolution of the Company.

Dissolution of the Bus Company.

(2) Any such order may provide for the disposal of any remaining property, rights or liabilities of the Company, and may contain such supplementary, incidental and consequential provisions as may appear to the Secretary of State to be necessary or expedient.

(3) Without prejudice to the generality of subsection (2) above, any such order may in particular make provision—

(a) for the preparation by such person or persons as may be specified in the order of a statement or statements of the Company's accounts for the period from the end of that dealt with in the last annual statement of accounts sent by the Company to the Secretary of State under section 24(3) of the 1962 Act down to the date of the dissolution of the Company ;

(b) for the auditing of any such statement of accounts ;

(c) for the making to the Secretary of State by such person or persons as may be specified in the order of a report or reports on the exercise and performance by the Company of their functions during any period not dealt with in the reports made by the Company under section 27(8) of the 1962 Act ;

(d) making such amendments or repeals in any provision of the 1962 Act or the 1968 Act or of this or any other Act as appear to the Secretary of State to be required in consequence of the dissolution of the Company.

(4) The Secretary of State may with the approval of the Treasury—

(a) pay to any person upon whom duties are imposed by virtue of subsection (3)(a) to (c) above such remuneration, and such allowances in respect of expenses, as the Secretary of State may with the agreement of the Treasury determine ; and

PART III

(b) incur expenditure in doing any other thing that falls to be done in preparation for or in connection with the dissolution of the Company.

(5) On the dissolution of the Company, any remaining right of the Secretary of State or liability of the Company in respect of the principal of or any interest on sums lent to the Company by the Secretary of State under section 20 of the 1962 Act shall be extinguished.

Reduction of assets of National Loans Fund.

55. The assets of the National Loans Fund shall be reduced by the aggregate amount by which the liability of the Bus Company in respect of the principal of or any interest on sums lent to the Company by the Secretary of State under section 20 of the 1962 Act is extinguished under section 53 or 54 of this Act.

Interpretation of Part III.

56. In this Part of this Act—

(a) references to the Bus Company shall be read in accordance with section 47(1) of this Act ; and

(b) " the Company's disposal programme " has the meaning given by subsection (4) of that section.

PART IV

LOCAL PASSENGER TRANSPORT SERVICES

Passenger Transport Areas

Passenger Transport Areas, Authorities and Executives.

57.—(1) In section 9 of the 1968 Act (designation of passenger transport areas and establishment of Passenger Transport Authorities and Executives)—

(a) for subsections (1) to (4) there shall be substituted the following subsections—

" (1) For the purposes of this Part of this Act—

(a) each of the following areas, that is to say—

(i) in England and Wales, the metropolitan counties ; and

(ii) in Scotland, that part of the Strathclyde region which was a designated area for the purposes of this Part of this Act immediately before the date on which section 57 of the Transport Act 1985 came into operation ;

shall be a passenger transport area ;

(b) the Passenger Transport Authority for a passenger transport area (referred to below in this Part of this Act, in relation to that area, as " the Authority ") shall be—

(i) in relation to a passenger transport area in England and Wales, the metropolitan county council ; and

(ii) in relation to the Strathclyde passenger transport area, the Strathclyde regional council ; and

(c) the Passenger Transport Executive for a passenger transport area (referred to below in this Part of this Act, in relation to that area, as " the Executive ") shall be the body which immediately before the date mentioned in paragraph (a) above was the Passenger Transport Executive for the designated area for the purposes of this Part of this Act corresponding to that passenger transport area.

(2) The Executive for a passenger transport area consists of—

(a) a Director General appointed in accordance with Part II of Schedule 5 to this Act by the Authority ; and

(b) not less than two nor more than eight other members so appointed by the Authority after consultation with the Director General.

(3) Subject to subsection (2) of this section and Part II of Schedule 5 to this Act, the Secretary of State may by order make with respect to the Executive for any passenger transport area—

(a) such provision with respect to any of the matters referred to in Part III of that Schedule ; and

(b) such supplementary, incidental and consequential provision ;

as appears to the Secretary of State to be necessary or expedient.

(4) Before making any order under subsection (3) of this section, the Secretary of State shall consult with the Passenger Transport Authority for the area and, where the area is in England and Wales, with the councils of the districts comprised in the area." ;

(b) in subsection (5), as it applies to England and Wales, for the words " constituent areas " there shall be substituted the words " the districts comprised in a passenger transport area " ;

(c) in subsection (5), as it applies to Scotland, for the word " designated " there shall be substituted the words " passenger transport " ; and (*d*) subsection (7) shall be omitted.

(2) After section 9 there shall be inserted the following sections—

" General
functions of
Passenger
Transport
Authorities
and
Executives.

9A.—(1) It shall be the duty of the Authority for any passenger transport area to formulate from time to time general policies with respect to the descriptions of public passenger transport services they consider it appropriate for the Executive for their area to secure for the purpose of meeting any public transport requirements within their area which in the view of the Authority would not be met apart from any action taken by the Executive for that purpose.

(2) The Authority shall seek and have regard to the advice of the Executive for their area in formulating their policies under subsection (1) of this section.

(3) It shall be the duty of the Executive for any passenger transport area to secure the provision of such public passenger transport services as they consider it appropriate to secure for meeting any public transport requirements within their area in accordance with policies formulated by the Authority for their area under subsection (1) of this section.

(4) The Executive shall have power to enter into an agreement providing for service subsidies for the purpose of securing the provision of any service under subsection (3) of this section ; but their power to do so—

(*a*) shall be exercisable only where the service in question would not be provided without subsidy ; and

(*b*) is subject to sections 89 to 92 of the Transport Act 1985 (tendering for local services, etc.).

(5) Where it appears to the Authority for any passenger transport area that it would be appropriate for the Executive for that area to take any measures for the purpose of or in connection with promoting, so far as relates to that area—

(*a*) the availability of public passenger transport services other than subsidised services and the operation of such services, in conjunction with each other and with any available subsidised services, so as to meet any public transport requirements the Authority consider it appropriate to meet ; or (*b*) the convenience of the public (including persons who are elderly or disabled) in using all available public passenger transport services (whether subsidised or not) ;

the Authority may from time to time formulate general policies with respect to the description of such measures to be taken by the Executive for that area, and the Executive shall take such measures for the purpose or in the connection mentioned above as appear to them to be appropriate for carrying out those policies.

(6) It shall be the duty—

(*a*) of the Authority for any passenger transport area, in formulating any such policies ; and

(*b*) of the Executive for any passenger transport area, in carrying out any such policies ;

so to conduct themselves as not to inhibit competition between persons providing or seeking to provide public passenger transport services in their area.

(7) It shall be the duty both of the Authority and of the Executive for any passenger transport area, in exercising or performing any of their functions under the preceding provisions of this section, to have regard to the transport needs of members of the public who are elderly or disabled.

(8) No person who is for the time being—

(*a*) the operator of any public passenger transport services ;

(*b*) a director of any company or (as the case may be) an employee of any company or other person who is such an operator ;

(*c*) a director or employee of any company which is a member of a group of interconnected bodies corporate any one or more of which is such an operator ;

(*b*) in Scotland, a regional or islands council.
be) an employee of a partner of such an operator ;

shall be appointed as a member, officer or servant of the Executive for any passenger transport area ; and any person so appointed who subsequently becomes such an operator, director, partner or employee shall immediately vacate his membership of the Executive, or (as the case may be) his office or employment with the Executive.

(9) References in subsection (5) above to subsidised services are references to services provided under an agreement providing for service subsidies entered into—

    (*a*) by the Executive for the area in question or for any other area under subsection (4) of this section ; or

    (*b*) by any non-metropolitan county or district council in England and Wales or by any regional or islands council in Scotland under section 63 of the Transport Act 1985.

(10) For the purposes of subsection (8) above, any two bodies corporate are to be treated as interconnected if one of them is a body corporate of which the other is a subsidiary or if both of them are subsidiaries of the same body corporate ; and in that subsection " group of interconnected bodies corporate " means a group consisting of two or more bodies corporate all of which are interconnected with each other in the sense given above.

(11) In this section and section 9B of this Act " public passenger transport services " has the same meaning as in the Transport Act 1985 ; and—

    (*a*) references in this section to agreements providing for service subsidies ; and

    (*b*) references in this section and that section to the operator of, or to persons operating, any public passenger transport services ;

shall be read as if contained in that Act.

Consultation and publicity with respect to policies as to services.

9B.—(1) When considering from time to time the formulation of policies for the purposes of section 9A(1) of this Act, the Authority for a passenger transport area shall consult—

    (*a*) with every Passenger Transport Authority, county council or regional council whose area may be affected by those policies ; and

    (*b*) either with persons operating public passenger transport services within their area or with organisations appearing to the Authority to be representative of such persons;

and where the passenger transport area is in England and Wales the Authority shall also consult with the councils of the districts comprised in that area about the requirements of transport arising out of or in connection with the exercise and performance by those councils of their functions as local education authorities or of their social services functions.

(2) As soon as practicable after any occasion when they formulate new or altered policies for those purposes, the Authority concerned shall publish a statement of all policies so formulated by them on that or any previous occasion which for the time being apply in relation to the performance by the Executive for their area of their duty to secure services under section 9A(3).

(3) When the Authority publish such a statement, they shall send a copy of the statement—

    (a) to each Authority or council whom they were required to consult under subsection (1)(a) above ; and

    (b) to each of the persons or (as the case may be) organisations whom they consulted under subsection (1)(b) above ;

in relation to the formulation of their policies on the occasion in question.

(4) The Authority shall also—

    (a) cause a copy of the statement last published by them under subsection (2) above to be made available for inspection (at all reasonable hours) at such places as they think fit ; and

    (b) give notice, by such means as they think expedient for bringing it to the attention of the public, as to the places at which a copy of that statement may be inspected."

(3) Section 20 of the 1968 Act (which imposes a special duty on the Executive for any passenger transport area to which that section is applied by an order made by the Secretary of State under subsection (1) of that section to secure by agreement with the Railways Board the provision of such railway passenger services as the Authority decide to be necessary to ensure a proper contribution towards the provision of a properly integrated and efficient system of public passenger transport to meet the needs of their area) shall apply in relation to the Executive for every passenger transport area ; and subsection (1) of that section shall accordingly cease to have effect.

C

(4) Without prejudice to section 17(2)(*b*) of the Interpretation Act 1978 (preservation of subordinate legislation) any order under section 9(1) of the 1968 Act or under section 202(4) of the 1972 Act (orders establishing Passenger Transport Executives) which applies in relation to a Passenger Transport Executive immediately before this section comes into force shall have effect, so far as it makes with respect to that Executive any such provision as is mentioned in section 9(3) (as substituted by subsection (1) above), as if made under that provision (as so substituted).

(5) Section 9A(8) of the 1968 Act shall not apply in relation to any person appointed before this section comes into force as a member, officer or servant of the Passenger Transport Executive for any passenger transport area.

(6) Schedule 3 to this Act shall have effect for the purpose of making amendments consequential on the provisions of this section in the 1968 Act and in the other enactments there mentioned.

Local
government
reorganisation:
transport
functions.
1985 c. 51.

58.—(1) The following provisions of this section, with the exception of subsection (5), shall have effect from the abolition date within the meaning of the Local Government Act 1985 (that is to say, 1st April 1986).

(2) In section 9 of the 1968 Act (as amended by section 57(1) of this Act)—

    (*a*) in subsection (1)—

        (i) at the beginning there shall be inserted the words " Subject to any order under section 42(1)(*c*) of the Local Government Act 1985 (alteration or abolition of passenger transport areas, etc.) "; and

        (ii) in paragraph (*b*)(i), for the word " council " there shall be substituted the words " passenger transport authority for the county which is coterminous with or includes that passenger transport area ";

    (*b*) in subsection (4), after the word " the " (where it last occurs) there shall be inserted the words " county which is coterminous with or includes that "; and

    (*c*) in subsection (5), as it applies in England and Wales, after the words " comprised in " there shall be inserted the words " a county which is coterminous with or includes ".

(3) In section 9B(1) of that Act, after the words " comprised in " there shall be inserted the words " the county which is coterminous with or includes ".

(4) In the Local Government Act 1985—

    (*a*) paragraphs 1, 2 and 4 of Schedule 12 shall be omitted;

(b) in section 39(2) (operative dates for Schedule 12), for the words " paragraphs 1 to 4 " there shall be substituted the words " paragraph 3 " ; and

(c) in section 42(1)(c) (reorganisation of functions with respect to passenger transport), after the words " section 39 above " there shall be inserted the words " or section 58 of the Transport Act 1985 ".

(5) Provisions of that Act referring generally to that Act, or to any provision made by or under that Act, shall have effect as if subsections (1) to (3) above were contained in that Act.

59.—(1) Before such date as the Secretary of State may Transfer specify in the case of any Passenger Transport Executive in a of bus direction given to that Executive, the Executive shall form a undertakings company for the purpose of carrying on— of Executives
  to companies
(a) activities of any description carried on by the Executive owned by in or for the purposes of the provision of any service Authorities. for the carriage of passengers by road currently provided by the Executive in exercise of any of their powers under section 10(1) of the 1968 Act ; and

(b) any activities which appear to the Executive to be incidental to or connected with any activities within paragraph (a) above or to be capable of being conveniently carried on in association with any such activities.

(2) The company shall be a company limited by shares registered under the Companies Act 1985. 1985 c. 6.

(3) Where the Executive for any passenger transport area have formed a company in pursuance of this section, the Executive shall, before such date as the Secretary of State may specify in a direction given to the Executive, submit to the Secretary of State a scheme providing for the transfer to the company of any property, rights or liabilities of the Executive, or of any wholly-owned subsidiary of theirs, which it appears to the Executive to be appropriate to transfer to that company.

(4) In preparing a scheme in pursuance of subsection (3) above, the Executive in question shall take into account any advice given by the Secretary of State as to the provisions he regards as appropriate for inclusion in the scheme (and in particular, but without prejudice to the generality of that, as to the description of property, rights and liabilities it is in his view appropriate to transfer to the company).

(5) A scheme under subsection (3) above shall not come into force until it has been approved by the Secretary of State or until such date as the Secretary of State may, in giving his approval, specify ; and the Secretary of State may approve a scheme either without modifications or with such modifications

as, after consultation with the Executive and with the Passenger Transport Authority for the area in question, he thinks fit.

(6) If the Secretary of State is not satisfied that a scheme submitted under subsection (3) above accords with any such advice given by him as is mentioned in subsection (4) above, or would do so with appropriate modifications, he may, after consultation with the Executive and with the Passenger Transport Authority for the area in question, instead of approving the scheme substitute for it a scheme of his own, to come into force on such date as may be specified in the scheme.

(7) On the coming into force of a scheme under this section the property, rights and liabilities affected by the scheme shall, subject to section 129 of this Act, be transferred and vest in accordance with the scheme.

(8) Following the transfer to the company under subsection (7) above of the property, rights and liabilities affected by the scheme, the Executive shall, before such date as the Secretary of State may specify in a direction given to the Executive, transfer all shares in or other securities of the company to the Passenger Transport Authority for their area.

(9) Where—

    (a) the property, rights and liabilities transferred under subsection (7) above include the whole of the undertaking of any wholly-owned subsidiary of the Executive ; and

    (b) it appears to the Executive that no further action is required on the part of that subsidiary to perfect any transfer under that subsection ;

the Executive shall secure that that subsidiary is wound up.

(10) Without prejudice to any other restriction on their powers, a Passenger Transport Executive may not dispose of any shares in or other securities of a company formed by that Executive in pursuance of this section otherwise than in accordance with subsection (8) above.

Exclusion of public sector co-operation requirements and bus operating powers.

60.—(1) This section applies where in the case of any passenger transport area a company (referred to below in this Part of this Act, in relation to that area, as " the initial company ") has been formed by the Passenger Transport Executive for that area (" the Executive ") in pursuance of section 59 of this Act.

(2) At any time after the Secretary of State has given to the Executive a direction under subsection (3) of that section the Secretary of State may by order provide that the Executive shall cease, on a day specified in the order, to be under the duty imposed by section 24(2) of the 1968 Act (duty to co-operate with the National Bus Company and the Scottish Transport Group and to enter into agreements for that purpose).

(3) Where an order is made under subsection (2) above, any duty of the National Bus Company and the Scottish Transport Group under section 24(2) of the 1968 Act to co-operate with the Executive (or with each other) shall cease on the day specified in the order to apply in relation to the Executive's area.

(4) Any order under subsection (2) above may include provision for the termination of any agreements made under section 24(2) to which the Executive are a party, on such terms and such dates as may be specified in relation to those agreements in the order (and different terms and dates may be so specified in relation to different agreements).

(5) At any time after the transfer required under section 59(8) of shares in or other securities of the initial company to the Passenger Transport Authority for the Executive's area has taken place the Secretary of State may by order provide that the Executive shall cease, on a day specified in the order, to have the powers under section 10(1)(i) and (viii) of the 1968 Act (powers to carry passengers by road and to let passenger vehicles on hire with or without trailers for the carriage of goods).

(6) Where an order is made under subsection (5) above in relation to the Executive, section 16(2) of the 1968 Act (which relates to the provision of special information in the annual report of Authorities and Executives as to certain businesses of providing services for the carriage of passengers by road) shall cease to apply in relation to any accounting period of the Executive beginning on or after the day specified in the order.

(7) The Secretary of State may by order provide for the repeal of—

    (a) section 24(2) of the 1968 Act ; and

    (b) section 10(1)(i) and (viii) of that Act ;

on the date on which, by virtue of the cumulative effect of orders made under this section, there ceases to be any Passenger Transport Executive in Great Britain who are under the duty imposed by section 24(2) or have the powers under section 10(1)(i) and (viii).

(8) Any order made under subsection (7) above may contain such supplementary, incidental and consequential provisions (including provisions modifying any enactment contained in this or any other Act) as may appear to the Secretary of State to be necessary or expedient in consequence of any repeals made by the order.

61.—(1) Where in the case of any passenger transport area the transfer required under section 59(8) of this Act of shares in or other securities of the initial company to the Passenger Transport Authority for that area has taken place, the Secretary

Division of undertakings of companies formed under section 59.

of State may by a direction given to that Authority require the Authority to submit to him in accordance with the following provisions of this section written proposals for the division of the undertaking of the initial company among two or more companies to be formed in pursuance of the proposals.

(2) Where the initial company has any wholly-owned subsidiaries, the proposals may, instead of or (as the case may be) in addition to providing for the transfer to any one or more of those companies of the shares in or other securities of any such subsidiary comprised in the initial company's undertaking, provide for—

(a) the division among those companies ; or

(b) the transfer to any one of them ;

of the whole or any part of the undertaking, or of any property, rights or liabilities, of that subsidiary.

(3) The proposals shall be submitted to the Secretary of State before the end of such period as may be specified in the direction.

(4) The proposals shall—

(a) provide for each company to be formed in pursuance of the proposals (referred to below in this section as a transferee company) to be a company limited by shares

1985 c. 6.   and registered under the Companies Act 1985 ;

(b) broadly describe the manner in which the undertaking of the initial company, and the whole or any part of the undertaking of any wholly-owned subsidiary of the initial company to which the proposals relate, is to be divided among the transferee companies or (as the case may be) transferred in accordance with the proposals to any one of those companies ; and

(c) provide for the winding up of the initial company, and of any wholly-owned subsidiary of the initial company the whole of whose undertaking is to be transferred in accordance with the proposals to any one or more of the transferee companies, on completion of the transfer of that company's or (as the case may be) of that subsidiary's undertaking.

(5) In preparing their proposals the Authority shall take into account any advice given by the Secretary of State as to the provisions he regards as appropriate for inclusion in the proposals (and in particular, but without prejudice to the generality of that, as to the description of property, rights and liabilities of the initial company and of any wholly-owned subsidiary of the initial company it is in his view appropriate to transfer to each of the transferee companies).

(6) The Secretary of State may approve the proposals either without modifications or with such modifications as, after consultation with the Authority, he thinks fit.

(7) If the Secretary of State is not satisfied that the proposals accord with any such advice given by him as is mentioned in subsection (5) above, or would do so with appropriate modifications, he may, after consultation with the Authority, instead of approving the proposals substitute for them a plan of his own.

(8) When the Secretary of State has approved the proposals or substituted for them a plan of his own, the Authority shall form each transferee company in accordance with the proposals as approved by the Secretary of State or (as the case may be) in accordance with the Secretary of State's plan, and secure the registration of that company under the Companies Act 1985, 1985 c. 6. before such date as the Secretary of State may specify in relation to that company in giving his approval to the proposals or (as the case may be) in that plan.

(9) When all the transferee companies have been formed in accordance with the proposals as so approved or (as the case may be) in accordance with the Secretary of State's plan, the Authority shall, before such date as the Secretary of State may specify in a direction given to the Authority, submit to the Secretary of State a scheme providing for the transfer to each transferee company of any property, rights and liabilities—

    (*a*) of the initial company ; and

    (*b*) of any wholly-owned subsidiary of the initial company ;

which are to be transferred in accordance with those proposals or (as the case may be) in accordance with that plan to that transferee company.

(10) A scheme under subsection (9) above shall not come into force until it has been approved by the Secretary of State or until such date as the Secretary of State may, in giving his approval, specify ; and the Secretary of State may approve a scheme either without modifications or with such modifications as, after consultation with the Authority, he thinks fit.

(11) On the coming into force of a scheme under subsection (9) above the property, rights and liabilities affected by the scheme shall, subject to section 129 of this Act, be transferred and vest in accordance with the scheme.

(12) When it appears to the Authority that no further action is required on the part of the initial company to perfect any transfer effected by the scheme, the Authority shall secure that the initial company is wound up in accordance with the proposals as approved by the Secretary of State or (as the case may be) in accordance with the Secretary of State's plan.

(13) Subsection (12) above shall apply in relation to any subsidiary of the initial company the whole of whose undertaking is transferred under the scheme to one or more of the transferee companies as it applies in relation to the initial company.

Protection of
employee
benefits on
transfer and
division of
bus
undertakings.

62.—(1) In this section, as it applies in relation to the Passenger Transport Executive or (as the case may be) in relation to the Passenger Transport Authority for any passenger transport area—

> " the first transfer " means the transfer under section 59(7) of this Act to the initial company of property, rights and liabilities of the Executive for that area ; and

> " the second transfer " means the transfer under section 61(11) of this Act to companies formed under that section of property, rights and liabilities of the initial company ;

and " the first transfer date " and " the second transfer date " mean respectively the date on which the first transfer and the date on which the second transfer takes effect.

(2) The Passenger Transport Executive for any passenger transport area shall have power to make, in such manner as they think fit, such provision as appears to them to be appropriate in connection with either the first or the second transfer for the maintenance to any extent of any concession, benefit or privilege of a description enjoyed immediately before the first transfer date by—

> (a) persons who then were or had been employed in such part of the Executive's undertaking, or of the undertaking of any wholly-owned subsidiary of the Executive, as was transferred on that date to the initial company ; or

> (b) members of the families of any such persons.

(3) Subject to subsection (4) below, the Passenger Transport Authority for any passenger transport area shall have power to make, in such manner as they think fit, such provision as appears to them to be appropriate in connection with the second transfer for the maintenance to any extent of any concession, benefit or privilege of a description enjoyed immediately before the second transfer date by—

> (a) persons who then were or had been employed in any undertaking or part of an undertaking transferred on that date to a company formed under section 61 of this Act ; or

> (b) members of the families of any such persons.

(4) Subsection (3) above shall not apply to any concession, benefit or privilege of a description to which subsection (2) above applies.

(5) Where provision for the maintenance of a concession, benefit or privilege of any description may be made under subsection (2) or (3) above provision may instead be made, in any cases or classes of case to which that subsection applies, for the making of any payment or the provision of any other concession, benefit or privilege in compensation for the loss or (as the case may be) for any reduction or limitation of concessions, benefits or privileges of that description.

Passenger transport in other areas

63.—(1) In each non-metropolitan county of England and Wales it shall be the duty of the county council—

(a) to secure the provision of such public passenger transport services as the council consider it appropriate to secure to meet any public transport requirements within the county which would not in their view be met apart from any action taken by them for that purpose ; and

(b) to formulate from time to time general policies as to the descriptions of services they propose to secure under paragraph (a) above.

(2) It shall be the duty of a regional or islands council in Scotland, in relation to any part of their area which is not a passenger transport area—

(a) to secure the provision of such public passenger transport services as the council consider it appropriate to secure to meet any public transport requirements within their area which would not in their view be met apart from any action taken by them for that purpose ; and

(b) to formulate from time to time general policies as to the descriptions of services they propose to secure under paragraph (a) above.

(3) In formulating policies under subsection (1)(b) or (2)(b) above with respect to the descriptions of services they propose to secure under subsection (1)(a) or (2)(a) above, a council shall have regard to any measures they are required or propose to take for meeting any transport requirements in exercise or performance of—

(a) any of their functions as a local education authority or (as the case may be) as an education authority ; or

(b) any of their social services or (as the case may be) social work functions.

(4) A non-metropolitan district council in England and Wales shall have power to secure the provision of such public passenger transport services as they consider it appropriate to secure

PART IV

Functions of local councils with respect to passenger transport in areas other than passenger transport areas.

to meet any public transport requirements within their area which would not in their view be met apart from any action taken by them for that purpose.

(5) For the purpose of securing the provision of any service under subsection (1)(*a*) or (2)(*a*) or (as the case may be) under subsection (4) above any council shall have power to enter into an agreement providing for service subsidies ; but their power to do so—

(*a*) shall be exercisable only where the service in question would not be provided without subsidy ; and

(*b*) is subject to sections 89 to 92 of this Act.

(6) A non-metropolitan county council in England and Wales or, in Scotland, a regional or islands council shall have power to take any measures that appear to them to be appropriate for the purpose of or in connection with promoting, so far as relates to their area—

(*a*) the availability of public passenger transport services other than subsidised services and the operation of such services, in conjunction with each other and with any available subsidised services, so as to meet any public transport requirements the council consider it appropriate to meet ; or

(*b*) the convenience of the public (including persons who are elderly or disabled) in using all available public passenger transport services (whether subsidised or not).

(7) It shall be the duty of a county council or (as the case may be) of a regional or islands council, in exercising their power under subsection (6) above, so to conduct themselves as not to inhibit competition between persons providing or seeking to provide public passenger transport services in their area.

(8) It shall be the duty of any council, in exercising or performing any of their functions under the preceding provisions of this section, to have regard to the transport needs of members of the public who are elderly or disabled.

(9) References in subsection (6) above to subsidised services are references to services provided under an agreement providing for service subsidies entered into—

(*a*) by the council in question or by any other county or district council or regional or islands council under this section ; or

(*b*) by the Passenger Transport Executive for any passenger transport area under section 9A(4) of the 1968 Act.

(10) In this Act—

(*a*) " public passenger transport services " means all those services on which members of the public rely for getting

from place to place, when not relying on private facilities of their own, including school transport but not—

  (i) services provided under permits under section
  19 of this Act, other than services provided wholly or
  mainly to meet the needs of members of the public
  who are elderly or disabled ; or

  (ii) excursions or tours ; and

(b) references, in relation to any Passenger Transport Executive, non-metropolitan county or district council or
regional or islands council, to agreements providing for
service subsidies are references to agreements under
which any person undertakes to provide a public passenger transport service of any description on terms
which include provision for the making of payments to
that person by that Executive or council.

64.—(1) When considering from time to time the formu- Consultation
lation of policies for the purposes of section 63(1)(b) or (2)(b) of and publicity
this Act, any council to whom either of those provisions applies with respect
shall consult— to policies as
to services.

(a) with every Passenger Transport Authority, county council or regional or islands council whose area may be
affected by those policies ; and

(b) either with persons operating public passenger transport
services within their area or with organisations appearing to the council to be representative of such persons ;

and where the council's area is in England and Wales the council shall also consult with the councils of districts comprised in
their area.

(2) As soon as practicable after any occasion when they
formulate new or altered policies for those purposes, any such
council shall publish a statement of all policies so formulated by
them on that or any previous occasion which they propose for
the time being to follow in the performance of their duty to
secure services under section 63(1)(a) or (as the case may be)
under section 63(2)(a).

(3) When any such council publish such a statement, they
shall send a copy of the statement—

(a) to each Authority or council whom they were required
to consult under subsection (1)(a) above ; and

(b) to each of the persons or (as the case may be) organisations whom they consulted under subsection (1)(b)
above ;

in relation to the formulation of their policies on the occasion in
question.

(4) The council shall also—

    (*a*) cause a copy of the statement last published by them under subsection (2) above to be made available for inspection (at all reasonable hours) at such places as they think fit ; and

    (*b*) give notice, by such means as they think expedient for bringing it to the attention of the public, as to the places at which a copy of that statement may be inspected.

Co-operation between certain councils and London Regional Transport.

65.—(1) Subject to the following provisions of this section, any non-metropolitan county or district council in England and Wales and London Regional Transport shall each have power to enter into any agreement or arrangements with the other under which that council or (as the case may be) London Regional Transport undertake to contribute towards any expenditure incurred by the other party to the agreement or arrangements in making payments to a person providing a public passenger transport service under any agreement entered into by that other party in exercise of any power that other party may have to secure the provision of that service.

(2) The agreement under which the payments are made must have been entered into in pursuance of the agreement or arrangements between the council in question and London Regional Transport.

1984 c. 32.

(3) The power of London Regional Transport under section 3(2) of the London Regional Transport Act 1984 (contracting-out powers) to enter into and carry out agreements with any person for the provision by that person of any public passenger transport service, if exercised in pursuance of any agreement or arrangements entered into under this section, shall be limited to cases where the service in question would not be provided without subsidy and shall also be subject to sections 89 to 92 of this Act.

(4) Section 28 of the London Regional Transport Act 1984 (agreements with respect to the provision by London Regional Transport of extra services and facilities financed by certain other authorities) shall cease to apply in relation to agreements with district councils, and accordingly—

    (*a*) in subsection (1) of that section—

        (i) the word " or " shall be inserted at the end of paragraph (*b*) ; and

        (ii) paragraph (*d*) and the word " or " immediately preceding it shall be omitted ; and

    (*b*) in subsection (2) of that section—

        (i) the word " and " shall be inserted after the word " borough " ; and

(ii) the words " and the council of any district " PART IV
shall be omitted.

(5) Subsection (3) above is without prejudice to section 6 of
the London Regional Transport Act 1984 (obligation of London 1984 c. 32.
Regional Transport to invite tenders for carrying on activities in
certain circumstances).

66.—(1) Subject to section 71 of this Act and subsection (2) Exclusion of
below, but notwithstanding anything in any other statutory pro- powers of
vision, a non-metropolitan district council in England and Wales certain
or, in Scotland, a regional council shall not have power to run bus
provide a service for the carriage of passengers by road which undertakings.
requires a PSV operator's licence.

(2) Subsection (1) above shall not have effect in relation to
any council who, at the time when this section comes into
force, are providing any such service until the end of such period
as may be specified by order made by the Secretary of State.

References below in this Part of this Act to a council operating a bus undertaking are references to any council to whom
this subsection applies.

(3) Any order under subsection (2) above may apply to all
councils within that subsection who are not for the time being
exempt by virtue of section 71 of this Act from subsection (1)
above, to any class of such councils, or to any such council
specified in the order ; and different periods may be specified
by any such order in relation to different councils or classes of
councils to whom it applies.

(4) Any order under subsection (2) above shall, in relation
to every period specified in the order for the purposes of that
subsection (" the primary period "), specify also a period ending before the primary period as the period allowed to councils
to whom the primary period applies for complying with such
of the requirements of sections 67 to 69 of this Act as are
applicable to them.

(5) A period specified by virtue of subsection (4) above in an
order under subsection (2) above is referred to in those sections,
in relation to any council to whom it applies, as the council's
preparatory period.

(6) Any order amending a previous order under subsection
(2) above, in so far as it extends any period specified in the
previous order for the purposes of that subsection, may be
framed so as to have effect from a date earlier than the making
of the order.

(7) For the purposes of this Part of this Act—

(*a*) a service for the carriage of passengers by road is a
service which requires a PSV operator's licence if

vehicles used in providing the service are used in such circumstances that a PSV operator's licence is required in respect of that use ;

(*b*) any council who have made (whether alone or jointly with any other authority or authorities) arrangements under any enactment for the discharge by any other authority or person of that council's functions with respect to the operation of any such service shall be taken to be providing that service at any time when it is being provided under those arrangements ; and

(*c*) references, in relation to any council operating a bus undertaking, to the council's bus undertaking are references (according to the context) to—

(i) all activities carried on, whether by the council themselves or by any other authority or person in pursuance of any such arrangements as are mentioned in paragraph (*b*) above or otherwise, in or for the purposes of the provision by the council of any such service ; or

(ii) all property of the council used or appropriated for use and all rights and liabilities of the council subsisting for the purposes of any such activities.

Formation of companies to run council bus undertakings.

67.—(1) Where an order is made under section 66(2) of this Act, the council or (as the case may be) each of the councils to whom the order applies shall, before the end of that council's preparatory period, form (whether alone or jointly with any other council operating a bus undertaking) one or more companies for the purpose of carrying on—

(*a*) activities of any description included among the activities of the bus undertaking of that council or (as the case may be) of any of the councils concerned in the formation of the company or companies in question ;

(*b*) activities of any other description included among the activities of any joint undertaking of which that council's bus undertaking, or (as the case may be) the bus undertaking of any council so concerned, forms part ; and

(*c*) any other activities which appear to the council or (as the case may be) to both or all of the councils so concerned to be incidental to or connected with any activities within paragraph (*a*) or (*b*) above or to be capable of being conveniently carried on in association with any such activities.

(2) Any company formed under this section shall be a company limited by shares registered under the Companies Act 1985.

1985 c. 6.

(3) Subject to subsections (4) and (5) below, a council's bus undertaking shall be regarded for the purposes of this Part of this Act as forming part of a joint undertaking if the services for the carriage of passengers by road provided in the course of the activities of the council's bus undertaking are wholly or mainly provided under any agreement for—

(a) the provision or operation of those services by a body acting on the joint behalf of that council and one or more other councils; or

(b) the operation of those services by any company operating those services in conjunction with services for the carriage of passengers by road provided by that company.

(4) Subsection (3)(a) above only applies where the agreement provides for the distribution among the parties on its termination of—

(a) all assets, or the proceeds of all assets, used or appropriated for use for the purpose of providing services for the carriage of passengers by road under the agreement; or

(b) all such assets or proceeds excluding only land or the proceeds of disposal of land.

(5) Subsection (3)(b) above only applies where—

(a) the agreement includes provision for securing that the parties on termination of the agreement hold shares of equal value in assets required to be brought into account on termination of the agreement; and

(b) those assets include all assets so used or appropriated for use.

(6) References in this Part of this Act, in relation to a council whose bus undertaking forms part of a joint undertaking, to the joint undertaking are references to all activities carried on, or (according to the context) to all property used or appropriated for use and all rights and liabilities subsisting for the purposes of any activities carried on, in pursuance of the agreement by reference to which that council falls within subsection (3) above.

68.—(1) Subject to subsection (2) below, a council to whom Schemes for section 67(1) of this Act applies shall, before the end of that transfer of council's preparatory period, submit to the Secretary of State a individual scheme providing for the transfer to a company or companies council bus undertakings formed by that council under that section of— to companies

(a) such of the property, rights and liabilities of the council formed under comprised in the council's bus undertaking; and section 67.

(b) such other property, rights and liabilities of the council; as it appears to the council to be appropriate to transfer to the company or companies in question.

(2) This section does not apply to a council whose bus undertaking forms part of a joint undertaking, except where any of the activities of the council's bus undertaking (" the separate activities ") are carried on by the council otherwise than in pursuance of any such agreement as is mentioned in section 67(3) of this Act; and in the latter case the reference in subsection (1)(*a*) above to property, rights and liabilities of the council shall be read as limited to property used or appropriated for use and rights and liabilities subsisting for the purposes of the separate activities.

(3) Two or more councils to whom this section applies may submit a joint scheme for the purposes of subsection (1) above; and in any such case the scheme may provide for the transfer of any property, rights and liabilities within that subsection as it applies to any one of those councils to a company or companies formed under section 67 of this Act by any other of those councils.

(4) In preparing a scheme for the purposes of subsection (1) above the council or councils concerned shall take into account any advice given by the Secretary of State as to the provisions he regards as appropriate for inclusion in the scheme (and in particular, but without prejudice to the generality of that, as to the description of property, rights and liabilities it is in his view appropriate to transfer to the company or companies in question).

(5) A scheme under this section shall not come into force until it has been approved by the Secretary of State or until such date as the Secretary of State may, in giving his approval, specify; and the Secretary of State may approve a scheme either without modifications or with such modifications as, after consultation with the council or councils concerned, he thinks fit.

(6) If the Secretary of State is not satisfied that a scheme submitted under subsection (1) above accords with any such advice given by him as is mentioned in subsection (4) above, or would do so with appropriate modifications, he may, after consultation with the council or councils concerned, instead of approving the scheme substitute for it a scheme of his own, to come into force on such date as may be specified in the scheme.

(7) On the coming into force of a scheme under this section, the property, rights and liabilities affected by the scheme shall, subject to section 129 of this Act, be transferred and vest in accordance with the scheme.

Orders for transfer of joint undertakings to companies formed under section 67.
69.—(1) This section applies to a council to whom section 67(1) of this Act applies whose bus undertaking forms part of a joint undertaking (referred to below in this section and in section 70 of this Act as a council participating in a joint undertaking).

(2) Any council participating in a joint undertaking shall, before the end of that council's preparatory period, submit to the Secretary of State written proposals for the transfer to a company or companies formed by that council under section 67 of—

(a) such of the property, rights and liabilities comprised in that council's share of the joint undertaking (whether or not then vested in that council) ; and

(b) such other property, rights and liabilities of the council ;

as it appears to the council to be appropriate to transfer to the company or companies in question.

(3) In any case within section 67(3)(a) of this Act both or all the councils participating in the joint undertaking may submit joint proposals for the purposes of subsection (2) above ; and in any such case the proposals—

(a) may relate to each council's share of the joint undertaking and (without prejudice to that) to all property, rights and liabilities of the body carrying on that undertaking ; and

(b) may provide for the transfer of any property, rights and liabilities within subsection (2) above as it applies to each of those councils to a company or companies formed under section 67 of this Act by any one or more of those councils.

(4) Any proposals submitted to the Secretary of State under this section must include proposals with respect to the terms on which the agreement under which the joint undertaking is carried on (referred to below in this section as the operating agreement) should be terminated.

(5) Individual proposals submitted to the Secretary of State under this section by a single council participating in a joint undertaking must include proposals for the division of that undertaking between the parties to it and the determination of the property, rights and liabilities to be allocated to each as his share.

(6) In preparing their proposals for the purposes of subsection (2) above the council or councils concerned shall take into account any advice given by the Secretary of State as to the provisions he regards as appropriate for inclusion in the proposals (and in particular, but without prejudice to the generality of that, as to the description of property, rights and liabilities it is in his view appropriate to transfer to the company or companies in question).

(7) Where in relation to any joint undertaking the Secretary of State has received under this section proposals submitted to

him (whether individually or jointly) by the council or (if more than one) by both or all of the councils participating in the undertaking, he shall, after considering those proposals and consulting the council or councils concerned, make an order in accordance with the following provisions of this section and section 70 of this Act.

(8) Before making such an order in any case within section 67(3)(*b*) of this Act the Secretary of State shall—

> (*a*) give the company carrying on the joint undertaking an opportunity of making written representations with respect to any proposals submitted to the Secretary of State in relation to that undertaking by the council concerned; and

> (*b*) consider any such representations made to him within such time as he may allow for the purpose.

(9) An order made by the Secretary of State under this section with respect to any joint undertaking may make provision—

> (*a*) where joint proposals were submitted under subsection (3) above with respect to that undertaking, for the transfer in accordance with the proposals of—

>> (i) all property, rights and liabilities of the body carrying on that undertaking; and

>> (ii) such of the property, rights and liabilities of the councils participating in the joint undertaking as may be specified in the order;

> (*b*) where individual proposals were submitted by any council participating in the joint undertaking, for the division of that undertaking between the parties to it and the determination of the property, rights and liabilities to be allocated to each as his share;

> (*c*) in a case within paragraph (*b*) above, for the transfer in accordance with the proposals submitted by any such council of—

>> (i) such of the property, rights and liabilities comprised in that council's share of the joint undertaking as determined by or under the order (whether or not then vested in that council) as may be specified in the order; and

>> (ii) such other property, rights and liabilities of that council as may be so specified;

> and, in any case within section 67(3)(*b*) of this Act, for the transfer to the company carrying on the joint undertaking of any property, rights and liabilities of the council concerned which are comprised in that company's share as determined by or under the order;

(*d*) for the transfer to such person as may be so specified from any council participating in the joint undertaking, or from the body carrying on the undertaking, of all such functions as may be determined by or under the order, being functions conferred or imposed on that council or body under any Act for the purposes of or in connection with the joint undertaking;

(*e*) for determining the effect of any transfer under the order in relation to persons employed in the joint undertaking or any part of it;

(*f*) for the protection of the interests of persons who by virtue of any transfer under the order fall to be treated as persons employed by the person taking that transfer;

(*g*) for the termination of the operating agreement on such terms as may be specified in the order; and

(*h*) in any case within section 67(3)(*a*) of this Act, for the dissolution of the body carrying on the joint undertaking.

(10) An order made by the Secretary of State under this section—

(*a*) may give effect to the proposals submitted to him under this section either without modifications or with such modifications as, after consultation with the council or councils concerned, the Secretary of State thinks fit; or

(*b*) if the Secretary of State is not satisfied that the proposals accord with any such advice given by him as is mentioned in subsection (6) above, or would do so with appropriate modifications, may make such provision in substitution for those proposals as the Secretary of State, after such consultation, thinks fit;

and references in subsection (9) above to an order's making provision for the transfer of any property, rights and liabilities in accordance with any such proposals shall be read as referring to those proposals as approved by the Secretary of State or to any provision made by the order by virtue of paragraph (*b*) above, as the case may require.

70.—(1) Any order under section 69 of this Act may contain such supplementary, incidental and consequential provisions as the Secretary of State thinks necessary or expedient for the purposes of the order, and in particular (but without prejudice to the generality of that) may include provision— Supplementary provisions with respect to orders under section 69.

(*a*) for the assumption by any council participating in the joint undertaking and by any person to whom any property, rights and liabilities are transferred under the order of such liabilities to one another as may be determined by or under the order to be appropriate having regard to the financial arrangements of that council before the severance from the other activities of the council of the joint undertaking or (as the case may be) of any activities of that council for the purposes of the joint undertaking;

(b) for the settlement by a court or otherwise of any dispute or other matter arising in connection with the order;

(c) for making in any statutory provision relating to, or to a class of undertakings which includes, the joint undertaking, such amendments or repeals as may appear to the Secretary of State to be required in consequence of any transfer under the order;

(d) for the making by any person to whom any property, rights and liabilities are transferred under the order to any council participating in the joint undertaking of payments by way of contributions to the cost of any adjustments arising from the severance mentioned in paragraph (a) above; and

(e) with respect to the consideration to be provided by any such person for any transfer under the order.

(2) Subject to subsection (3) below, any property, rights and liabilities for the transfer of which provision is made by an order under section 69 of this Act shall be transferred and vest in accordance with the order on such date or dates as may be appointed by the order for that purpose.

(3) Subject to the following provisions of this section, Schedule 4 to the 1968 Act (supplementary provisions as to certain transfers of property, rights and liabilities) shall apply to any transfer under subsection (2) above; and subsection (2) above shall have effect subject to the provisions of that Schedule.

(4) In Schedule 4 as it applies by virtue of subsection (3) above—

(a) any reference to a transfer by or a vesting by virtue of that Act shall be read as a reference to a transfer by or a vesting by virtue of the order; and

(b) the reference in paragraph 13(5) to the relevant provisions of that Act shall be read as including a reference to the relevant provisions of this Act.

(5) Any order under section 69 of this Act may make modifications in Schedule 4 for the purposes of its application to a transfer effected by that order.

PART IV
Exemption
for councils
running small
bus
undertakings.

71.—(1) Where in the case of any council operating a bus undertaking the number of vehicles owned by the council and used or appropriated for use in providing any service for the carriage of passengers by road which requires a PSV operator's licence does not exceed such number as may be specified by order made by the Secretary of State, the Secretary of State may on the application of that council grant to that council an exemption from section 66(1) of this Act for such period and on such terms and conditions as he thinks fit.

(2) Any such exemption shall cease to have effect if any term or condition applicable to it is contravened.

(3) Where a council operating a bus undertaking is in possession of a vehicle under an agreement for hire, hire-purchase, conditional sale or loan, that vehicle shall be treated for the purposes of subsection (1) above as owned by the council.

Further provisions with respect to companies formed under Part IV

The public
transport
companies
and their
controlling
authorities.

72. (1) References in this Part of this Act to a public transport company are references to any of the following—

(a) any company which was formed under section 59 of this Act by the Passenger Transport Executive for any passenger transport area and is for the time being a subsidiary of that Executive or of the Passenger Transport Authority for that area ;

(b) any company which was formed under section 61 of this Act by the Passenger Transport Authority for any passenger transport area and is for the time being a subsidiary of that Authority ; and

(c) any company which was formed by one or more councils under section 67 of this Act and is for the time being under local authority control.

(2) A company formed under section 67 of this Act shall be treated for the purposes of subsection (1)(c) above as under local authority control at any time when either—

(a) it is a subsidiary of a single district council in England and Wales or, in Scotland, of a single regional council ; or

(b) if two or more such councils who are members of the company were a single body corporate, it would be a subsidiary of that body corporate.

(3) References in this Part of this Act to a public transport company's controlling authority—

(a) in relation to a company within subsection (1)(a) or (b) above, are references to the Passenger Transport Executive or (as the case may be) the Passenger Transport Authority of whom it is a subsidiary ; and (*b*) in relation to a company within subsection (1)(c) above, are references to the council or councils referred to in subsection (2) above.

(4) References in this Part of this Act to a composite authority are references to a controlling authority consisting of two or more such councils as are referred to in subsection (2) above, and the councils concerned are referred to as the component councils of that authority.

(5) For the purposes of this Part of this Act a public transport company is an associated company—

    (*a*) in relation to a Passenger Transport Authority if that Authority or the Passenger Transport Executive for that Authority's area are its controlling authority ;

    (*b*) in relation to a Passenger Transport Executive if that Executive or the Passenger Transport Authority for that Executive's area are its controlling authority ; and

    (*c*) in relation to a district council in England and Wales or, in Scotland, a regional council, if that council are its controlling authority or one of the component councils of a composite authority who are its controlling authority.

Control over constitution and activities of public transport companies.

73.—(1) It shall be the duty of any public transport company's controlling authority to exercise their control over that company so as to ensure that the directors of the company include no more than the permitted maximum number of persons who are not full-time employees of the company.

(2) Following the transfer to a public transport company of its initial undertaking, it shall be the duty of that company's controlling authority to exercise their control over that company so as to ensure that the directors of the company include not less than the required minimum number of persons who are full-time employees of the company holding positions of responsibility for the management of the company's business or any part of it.

The reference above in this subsection to the transfer to a public transport company of its initial undertaking is a reference, in relation to any such company, to the transfer or (if more than one) the first transfer of property, rights and liabilities to that company under section 59(7), 61(11), 68(7) or 70(2) of this Act.

(3) Subject to subsection (5) below, it shall be the duty of any public transport company's controlling authority to exercise their control over the company so as to ensure that the company—

    (*a*) does not engage in activities in which the controlling authority have no power to engage or permit any body corporate which is its subsidiary to engage in any such activities;

(b) does not—

(i) borrow money from any person other than the controlling authority; or

(ii) permit any body corporate which is its subsidiary to borrow money from any person other than the company, any other subsidiary of the company, or the controlling authority;

with the exception in each case of borrowing by way of temporary loan or overdraft; and

(c) does not—

(i) raise money by the issue of shares or stock to any person other than the controlling authority; or

(ii) permit any body corporate which is its subsidiary to raise money by the issue of shares or stock to any person other than the company.

(4) Where a public transport company's controlling authority are a composite authority, the duties imposed by the preceding provisions of this section are joint duties of both or all of the component councils of that authority; and subsection (3) above shall apply in any such case as if—

(a) paragraph (a) referred to activities in which none of the component councils have power to engage; and

(b) references in paragraphs (b) and (c) to the controlling authority were references to the component councils.

(5) Subsection (3)(a) above shall not apply—

(a) in the case of a public transport company whose controlling authority are the Passenger Transport Authority for any passenger transport area, in relation to activities within the powers of the Executive for that area or activities which were formerly within those powers but have ceased to be so by virtue of any order made under section 60 of this Act;

(b) in the case of a public transport company within section 72(1)(c) of this Act, in relation to activities which were formerly within the powers of the council who formed or of any council who participated in forming that company, but have ceased to be so by virtue of section 66(1) of this Act.

(6) The Secretary of State may by order prescribe—

(a) the permitted maximum number for the purposes of subsection (1) above; and

(b) the required minimum number for the purposes of subsection (2) above.

PART IV
Disabilities of
directors of
public
transport
companies.

74.—(1) A director of a public transport company who is paid for acting as such or is an employee of the public transport company or a subsidiary of the public transport company shall be disqualified for being elected or being a member—

> (*a*) of any council who are that company's controlling authority ; or
>
> (*b*) where that company's controlling authority are a composite authority, of any of the component councils.

(2) Where a public transport company's controlling authority are a Passenger Transport Authority for a passenger transport area in England and Wales, a director of that company who is paid for acting as such or is an employee of that company or a subsidiary of that company shall be disqualified for being appointed or being a member of that Passenger Transport Authority.

(3) Subject to the following provisions of this section, if a director of a public transport company is a member of any such council as is mentioned in subsection (1)(*a*) or (*b*) above or of any such Passenger Transport Authority as is mentioned in subsection (2) above he shall not at any meeting of that council or Authority—

> (*a*) take part in the consideration or discussion of any contract or proposed contract with, or any other matter relating to the activities of, the public transport company or a subsidiary of that company ; or
>
> (*b*) vote on any question with respect to any such contract, proposed contract or other matter.

(4) The Secretary of State may grant a written dispensation from subsection (3) above in the case of any individual member.

(5) Any such dispensation—

> (*a*) may extend both to the consideration or discussion of any such contract, proposed contract or other matter and to voting with respect to it, or to either alone ;
>
> (*b*) may relate to contracts, proposed contracts or other matters of all descriptions or of any particular description specified in the dispensation ; and
>
> (*c*) may be withdrawn or varied at any time by a notice in writing given by the Secretary of State to the member in question.

(6) The Secretary of State may confer exemptions from subsection (3) above either generally or in the case of any class or description of members ; and—

> (*a*) subsection (5)(*a*) and (*b*) above shall apply in relation to any such exemption as they apply in relation to any

dispensation that may be granted under subsection (4) above ; and

    (b) any such exemption may be withdrawn or varied at any time by the Secretary of State.

(7) If any person fails to comply with subsection (3) above he shall for each offence be liable on summary conviction to a fine not exceeding level 4 on the standard scale, unless he proves that he did not know that a contract or proposed contract with, or any other matter relating to the activities of, the company concerned was the subject of consideration at the meeting in question.

(8) A prosecution for an offence under this section shall not, in England and Wales, be instituted except by or on behalf of the Director of Public Prosecutions.

(9) A council who are a public transport company's controlling authority or one of the component councils of such an authority, and any Passenger Transport Authority for a passenger transport area in England and Wales who are a public transport company's controlling authority, may by standing orders provide for the exclusion of a member of that council or Authority who is a director of that company from a meeting of that council or Authority while any contract or proposed contract with, or any other matter relating to the activities of, the public transport company or a subsidiary of that company is under consideration.

(10) Subsections (3) and (9) above shall apply as respects members of—

    (a) a committee of any such council or Passenger Transport Authority as is mentioned in subsection (9) above ; or

    (b) a joint committee of two or more local authorities one or more of whom is such a council or Passenger Transport Authority ;

(including in either case a sub-committee), as they apply in respect of members of that council or Authority, but with the substitution of references to meetings of any such committee for references to meetings of that council or Authority.

(11) In subsection (10)(b) above, " local authority "—

    (a) as respects England and Wales, has the same meaning as in the 1972 Act, except that it includes also a metropolitan county passenger transport authority ; and

    (b) as respects Scotland, has the same meaning as in the Local Government (Scotland) Act 1973.

1973 c. 65.

(12) For the purposes of section 94 of the 1972 Act or section 38 of the Local Government (Scotland) Act 1973 (disability of members of authorities for voting on account of interest in

contracts, etc.) a member of any such council or Passenger Transport Authority as is mentioned in subsection (9) above who is a director of the public transport company in question shall not be treated as having a pecuniary interest in any contract or proposed contract with, or in any other matter relating to the activities of, the public transport company or a subsidiary of that company by reason only of any interest of his in that company or in a subsidiary of that company.

(13) The provisions of this section shall apply in relation to a director of a subsidiary of a public transport company as they apply in relation to a director of such a company.

Powers of investment and disposal in relation to public transport companies.

75.—(1) Without prejudice to the powers of a Passenger Transport Executive, a Passenger Transport Authority or a district or regional council—

(a) to subscribe for shares on formation of a company formed by them (whether alone or jointly with any other council) in pursuance of any provision of this Part of this Act; or

(b) to acquire any shares in or other securities of a company so formed by way of consideration for any transfer of property, rights and liabilities to that company required or authorised under any such provision;

any such Authority or council shall have power at any time to subscribe for, take up or acquire (as the case may be) any shares in or other securities of any associated company.

(2) Any such Authority or council shall each have power to provide for the disposal, in such manner as they think fit, of any such shares or other securities.

(3) The exercise of the power under subsection (1) or (2) above requires the consent of the Secretary of State; and a public transport company's controlling authority may not, without that consent, in exercise of their control over that company permit—

(a) the disposal by that company of the whole of that company's undertaking;

(b) any disposal by that company of any shares in or other securities of a body corporate which is that company's subsidiary; or

(c) any disposal by that company of any part of that company's undertaking, or of any assets of that company (other than shares or securities within paragraph (b) above) which appears to that authority (or, in the case of a composite authority, to both or all of the component councils) to affect materially the structure of the company's business.

(4) A Passenger Transport Authority or a district or regional council who are a public transport company's controlling authority or (as the case may be) both or all of the component councils of a composite authority who are a public transport company's controlling authority, may, in exercising their power under subsection (2) above in relation to the disposal of any shares in or other securities of that company, provide for an employees' share scheme to be established in respect of that company; and any such scheme may provide for the transfer of shares without consideration.

76.—(1) It shall be the duty of any public transport company's controlling authority to exercise their control over that company so as to ensure that the company appoints only auditors who, in addition to being qualified for appointment as such auditors in accordance with section 389 of the Companies Act 1985, are approved for appointment as auditors of that company by the Audit Commission for Local Authorities in England and Wales.

Audit of accounts of public transport companies.

1985 c. 6.

(2) Where a public transport company's controlling authority are a composite authority, the duty imposed by subsection (1) above is a joint duty of both or all of the component councils of that authority.

(3) This section shall not apply to Scotland.

77.—(1) Any liability to meet capital expenses incurred by a public transport company shall be treated for the purposes of section 94 of the Local Government (Scotland) Act 1973 (consent of Secretary of State required for the incurring of liability to meet capital expenses) as a liability to meet capital expenses incurred by that company's controlling authority.

Local authority financial controls in Scotland.

1973 c. 65.

(2) Subject to the following provisions of this section, it shall be the duty of any public transport company's controlling authority to exercise their control over that company so as to ensure that the company shall appoint only auditors who, in addition to being qualified for appointment as such auditors in accordance with section 389 of the Companies Act 1985, are approved for appointment as auditors of the company by the Commission for Local Authority Accounts in Scotland.

(3) Where a public transport company's controlling authority are a Passenger Transport Executive, the reference in subsection (1) above to the controlling authority shall be read, in relation to that company, as a reference to the Passenger Transport Authority for that Executive's area.

(4) References in this section to a public transport company include references to any subsidiary of such a company.

(5) This section applies to Scotland only.

78.—(1) A Passenger Transport Executive and a district council or, in Scotland, a regional council shall each have power to enter into an agreement with any associated company, or with any subsidiary of an associated company, for the provision by that Executive or council for that company or (as the case may be) for that subsidiary of any administrative, professional or technical services.

(2) Any agreement under this section shall include provision for payment of proper commercial charges in respect of services to be provided under the agreement.

Financial
backing for
establishment
and operations
of public
transport
companies.

79.—(1) A Passenger Transport Authority and a district council or, in Scotland, a regional council shall each have power to make loans to any associated company, or to guarantee loans made to any associated company by any other person, for the provision of working capital.

(2) The reference in subsection (1) above to guaranteeing loans is a reference to guaranteeing the repayment of the principal of, the payment of interest on, and the discharge of any other financial obligation in connection with, any such loans.

(3) The exercise of the power under subsection (1) above, otherwise than in pursuance of any provision made by any scheme or order under this Part of this Act in connection with any transfer of property, rights and liabilities to the company in question for which that scheme or order provides, requires the consent of the Secretary of State.

(4) A Passenger Transport Authority and a district council or, in Scotland, a regional council shall each have power to make loans—

(a) to any associated company ; or

(b) to any subsidiary of an associated company ;

for the purpose of meeting any expenses incurred or to be incurred by that company or subsidiary in connection with the provision or improvement of assets in connection with its business.

(5) Any loan under subsection (4) above must be made on terms, both as to rates of interest and otherwise, no more favourable than the terms on which the authority making the loan would themselves be able to borrow at the time when the loan is made.

(6) A Passenger Transport Authority and a district council or, in Scotland, a regional council shall each have power to give any guarantees and do any other things which appear

to that Authority or (as the case may be) to that council to be
necessary or expedient for the purpose of or in connection with—

  (a) any disposal authorised by section 75(2) of this Act ;
      or

  (b) any disposal by any associated company of the whole
      or any part of that company's undertaking, or of any
      property, rights or liabilities of that company.

(7) Where any such disposal requires or (as the case may be)
may not be permitted without the consent of the Secretary of
State, the power under subsection (6) above may not be exercised in relation to that disposal without the consent of the
Secretary of State.

(8) Subject to subsection (9) below, a Passenger Transport
Authority and a district council or, in Scotland, a regional council shall each have power, with the consent of the Secretary of
State, to provide financial assistance by way of grants, loans or
guarantees for any associated company which has incurred
losses affecting the viability of its business.

(9) The power under subsection (8) above may only be exercised for the purpose of any plan approved by the Secretary of
State for improving the efficiency of the company's operations
and its commercial performance generally so as to enable it
to carry on business without further assistance from the Authority or council concerned or from any other council who are a
member of the company.

(10) A Passenger Transport Authority and a district council
or, in Scotland, a regional council shall each have power, where
on the winding up of any associated company the assets of the
company are not sufficient to meet the company's liabilities, to
make to the creditors of the company such payments as may
be necessary to meet the balance of those liabilities (and may
accordingly give to persons dealing or proposing to deal with
any such company such guarantees with respect to the exercise
of their power under this subsection in relation to that company
as they think fit).

Miscellaneous and supplementary

80. A Passenger Transport Authority, in exercising their func- Duty of
tions— Passenger
  Transport
  (a) in relation to the formation of companies under section Authority not
      61 of this Act and the formulation of proposals under to inhibit
      that section ; competition.

  (b) in relation generally to the exercise of rights in rela-
      tion to any public transport company arising from the
      holding of any shares in or other securities of that
      company ;

(c) in relation in particular to the exercise of control by virtue of any such rights over any disposal by any such company of the whole or any part of that company's undertaking, or of any property, rights or liabilities of that company ; and

(d) in relation to any disposal under section 75(2) of this Act ;

shall so conduct themselves as not to inhibit competition between persons providing or seeking to provide public passenger transport services in their area.

81.—(1) A Passenger Transport Executive for any passenger transport area shall have power—

(a) to provide bus stations and associated facilities at any place in or in the vicinity of their area ; and

(b) to maintain, repair and operate bus stations and associated facilities provided under paragraph (a) above or under their former powers.

(2) Where a council who, at the time when section 66 of this Act comes into force, are providing a service for the carriage of passengers by road which requires a PSV operator's licence, have ceased by virtue of subsection (1) of that section to have power to provide such a service, that council shall have power to maintain, repair and operate bus stations and associated facilities provided by them under their former powers.

(3) Any charges for the use of accommodation for public service vehicles at any bus station provided by the Passenger Transport Executive for any passenger transport area or provided by any other person under any agreement entered into by any such Executive under section 10(1)(xv) of the 1968 Act (contracting-out powers) shall be reasonable.

(4) Subsection (3) above only applies where the charges are made by the Executive in question under section 10(1)(xiii) of that Act or by a person who is operating the bus station under any such agreement otherwise than as agent for the Executive.

(5) Any such council as is mentioned in subsection (2) above shall have power—

(a) to make reasonable charges for the use of accommodation for public service vehicles at any bus station provided under their former powers ; and

(b) to make reasonable charges for the use of, or let on hire to any person, any associated facilities provided by them in connection with any bus station so provided.

(6) If any person who is the holder of a PSV operator's licence in respect of any vehicles using accommodation for public service

vehicles at any such bus station as is mentioned in subsection (3) or (5) above considers that charges for the use of that accommodation are unreasonable, that person may apply to the traffic commissioner for the traffic area in which the bus station is situated (or, where it is situated partly in one area and partly in another, to the traffic commissioner for such of those areas as may be agreed between the traffic commissioners concerned or, in default of agreement, determined by the Secretary of State).

(7) On any application under subsection (6) above the traffic commissioner may determine the charges to be made in respect of the applicant's vehicles for such period and on such terms as he thinks fit.

82.—(1) Neither a Passenger Transport Executive nor a local authority shall, in the exercise of any of their powers— Bus stations: restrictions on discriminatory practices, etc.

> (*a*) in relation to the provision or operation of bus stations or any associated facilities; or
>
> (*b*) (without prejudice to paragraph (*a*) above) in relation in particular to the charges to be made for the use of any accommodation at a bus station or of any associated facilities ;

act in such a way as to discriminate (whether directly or indirectly) against any holder, or class of holder, of a PSV operator's licence.

(2) In relation to a local authority, the powers in question under subsection (1) above include in particular (without prejudice to the generality of that subsection) their powers under section 38 of the Road Traffic Regulation Act 1984 (appointment of parking places provided under section 32 of that Act as stations for public service vehicles and provision of accommodation in connection with places so appointed). 1984 c. 27.

(3) Where under any agreement (other than an agency agreement) entered into by a Passenger Transport Executive under section 10(1)(xv) of the 1968 Act (contracting-out powers) a person is operating a bus station or any associated facilities provided by that Executive or provided by that or any other person under any such agreement, that person shall not—

> (*a*) in relation to the operation of that bus station or (as the case may be) of those facilities ; or
>
> (*b*) (without prejudice to paragraph (*a*) above) in relation in particular to the charges to be made for the use of any accommodation at that station or (as the case may be) for the use of those facilities ;

act in such a way as to discriminate (whether directly or indirectly) against any holder, or class of holder, of a PSV operator's licence.

(4) The reservation of the whole or any part of the accommodation for public service vehicles at any bus station for such vehicles used in providing local services or (as the case may be) for such vehicles used in providing services other than local services shall not be taken to be discrimination prohibited by subsection (1) or (3) above.

1983 c. 10.

(5) Notwithstanding anything in section 8 of the Transport Act 1983 (obligation to accept tenders for carrying on activities of Executives in certain circumstances) a Passenger Transport Executive may not in exercise of their powers under section 10(1)(xv) of the 1968 Act enter into an agreement (other than an agency agreement) for—

> (a) the provision of any bus station or associated facilities the Executive have power under section 81 of this Act to provide ; or

> (b) the operation of any bus station or associated facilities provided by the Executive under that section or under their former powers or provided by any other person under any agreement entered into by the Executive under section 10(1)(xv) ;

by a person who is the operator of any public passenger transport services or a person connected with any such operator.

(6) In this section " agency agreement " means, in relation to any agreement under section 10(1)(xv), an agreement with any person for the carrying on of activities by that person as agent for the Executive concerned.

(7) Any such agreement as is mentioned in subsection (5)(b) above entered into after this subsection comes into force shall include provision for ensuring that it will come to an end if the person who under the agreement is to operate the bus station or associated facilities to which it applies becomes the operator of any public passenger transport services or a person connected with any such operator.

(8) On and after the date on which this section comes into force, subsection (5) above shall apply in relation to any such agreement as is there mentioned entered into by the Passenger Transport Executive for any passenger transport area before that date as if this section had come into force on 11th July 1985.

Provisions
supplementary
to sections 81
and 82.

83.—(1) References in section 81 of this Act to the former powers of any such council as is mentioned in subsection (2) of that section are references to any powers which have ceased to be exercisable by that council by virtue of the application to that council of section 66(1) of this Act ; and references in that section and in section 82 of this Act to the former powers of a Passenger Transport Executive are references to any powers which have ceased to be exercisable by that Executive by virtue of any order PART IV under section 60(5) of this Act.

(2) For the purposes of section 82 of this Act a person is a person connected with the operator of any public passenger transport services if that person is a member of a group of interconnected bodies corporate any one or more of which is such an operator.

(3) For the purposes of subsection (2) above, any two bodies corporate are to be treated as interconnected if one of them is a body corporate of which the other is a subsidiary or if both of them are subsidiaries of the same body corporate ; and in that subsection " group of interconnected bodies corporate " means a group consisting of two or more bodies corporate all of which are interconnected with each other in the sense given above.

(4) In section 82 of this Act " local authority " means—

(a) in relation to England and Wales, the council of a county, London borough or district or the Common Council of the City of London ; and

(b) in relation to Scotland, a regional or islands council.

(5) In sections 81 and 82 of this Act and this section—

(a) " bus station " means a parking place which may be used by public service vehicles (including any such parking place which forms part of any interchange facilities for enabling passengers travelling by one means of transport to continue their journey by another) ; and

(b) " associated facilities " means, in relation to a bus station, any amenities or facilities provided for use in connection with that station.

84.—(1) Regulations may provide for the payment, by such Compensation persons as may be prescribed by or determined under the regu- for loss of lations, in such cases and to such extent as may be so pre- employment, scribed or determined, of pensions, allowances or gratuities by etc. way of compensation to or in respect of persons who have suffered loss of employment or loss or diminution of emoluments or pension rights by reason of—

(a) the disposal under section 75(2) of this Act of any interests held by a Passenger Transport Authority or district or regional council in a public transport company ;

(b) the disposal by any such company of the whole or any part of that company's undertaking ; or

(c) any transfer of property, rights and liabilities under section 59, 61, 68 or 70 of this Act.

D

(2) Regulations under this section may—

    (a) include provision as to the manner in which and the persons to whom any claim for compensation is to be made, and for the determination of all questions arising under the regulations;

    (b) make or authorise the Secretary of State to make exceptions and conditions in relation to any classes of persons or any circumstances to which the regulations apply; and

    (c) be framed so as to have effect from a date earlier than the making of the regulations;

but regulations having effect from a date earlier than their making shall not place any individual who is qualified to participate in the benefits for which the regulations provide in a worse position than he would have been in if the regulations had been so framed as to have effect only from the date of their making.

(3) Regulations under this section may include all or any of the following provisions, namely—

    (a) provision authorising the payment, without probate or, in Scotland, confirmation, and without other proof of title, of any sum due under the regulations in respect of a person who has died to his personal representatives or such other persons as may be prescribed by the regulations;

    (b) provision rendering void any assignment or, in Scotland, assignation of or charge on, or any agreement to assign or charge, any benefit under the regulations, and provision that on the bankruptcy of or, in Scotland, sequestration of the estate of, or granting of a trust deed for creditors by, a person entitled to such a benefit no part of it shall pass to any trustee or other person acting on behalf of the creditors except in accordance with an order made by a court in pursuance of any enactment specified in the regulations; and

    (c) such incidental, supplementary, consequential and transitional provisions as appear to the Secretary of State to be necessary or expedient.

(4) Subject to subsection (5) below, where regulations under this section have made provision for the payment of pensions, allowances or gratuities as mentioned in subsection (1) above, compensation in respect of any such loss of employment or loss or diminution of emoluments or pension rights as is mentioned in that subsection shall be paid only in accordance with those regulations in any case to which those regulations apply; and accordingly such compensation shall not be paid under any other

statutory provision, by virtue of any provision in a contract or otherwise.

(5) Subsection (4) above shall not prevent any person from making any payment to which a person is entitled by virtue of contractual rights acquired by him before such date as the Secretary of State may by order specify.

85.—(1) The Secretary of State may by order make provision for the transfer of all functions, property, rights and liabilities of the Passenger Transport Executive for any passenger transport area specified in the order to the Passenger Transport Authority for that area.   Incorporation of Passenger Transport Executives in Authorities for their area.

(2) An order under this section may contain such supplementary, incidental and consequential provisions as may appear to the Secretary of State to be necessary or expedient.

(3) Without prejudice to the generality of subsection (2) above, any such order may, in particular—

(a) provide for enactments relating to the functions of Passenger Transport Executives and Authorities respectively to have effect in relation to the passenger transport area specified in the order with such modifications as may be so specified ; and

(b) provide for the dissolution of the Passenger Transport Executive for that area.

(4) The property, rights and liabilities to which an order under this section relates shall, subject to subsection (5) below, be transferred and vest in accordance with the order on such date as may be appointed by the order for that purpose.

(5) Subject to the following provisions of this section, Schedule 4 to the 1968 Act shall apply to any transfer under subsection (4) above ; and subsection (4) above shall have effect subject to the provisions of that Schedule.

(6) In Schedule 4 as it applies by virtue of subsection (5) above—

(a) any reference to a transfer by or a vesting by virtue of that Act shall be read as a reference to a transfer by or a vesting by virtue of the order ; and

(b) the reference in paragraph 13(5) to the relevant provisions of that Act shall be read as including a reference to the relevant provisions of this Act.

(7) Any order under this section may make modifications in Schedule 4 for the purposes of its application to a transfer effected by that order.

PART IV

(8) No order shall be made under this section unless a draft of the order has been laid before, and approved by a resolution of, each House of Parliament.

Amendments consequential on orders under section 85.

86.—(1) The Secretary of State may by order provide for the modifications in the enactments mentioned in section 85(3)(*a*) of this Act, as those modifications apply for the time being in relation to passenger transport areas to which an order under that section applies, to have general effect on the date on which, by virtue of the cumulative effect of orders under that section, they first have effect in relation to all such areas in Great Britain.

(2) Any order made under this section may contain such supplementary, incidental and consequential provisions (including provisions modifying any enactments contained in this or any other Act) as may appear to the Secretary of State to be necessary or expedient in consequence of giving general effect to the modifications mentioned in subsection (1) above.

Interpretation of Part IV.

87. In this Part of this Act—

> (*a*) references to the initial company shall be read, in relation to any passenger transport area, in accordance with section 60(1) of this Act;
>
> (*b*) references to a council operating a bus undertaking shall be read in accordance with section 66(2) of this Act;
>
> (*c*) references to—
>
>> (i) a service for the carriage of passengers by road which requires a PSV operator's licence;
>>
>> (ii) the provision of any such service by any council; and
>>
>> (iii) the bus undertaking of any council operating a bus undertaking;
>
> shall be read in accordance with the relevant provisions of section 66(7) of this Act;
>
> (*d*) references to a joint undertaking of which any council's bus undertaking forms part shall be read in accordance with section 67(6) of this Act; and
>
> (*e*) references to—
>
>> (i) a public transport company;
>>
>> (ii) a public transport company's controlling authority;
>>
>> (iii) a composite authority;
>>
>> (iv) component councils of a composite authority; and
>>
>> (v) an associated company;
>
> shall be read in accordance with the relevant provisions of section 72 of this Act.

PART V

FINANCIAL PROVISIONS

Expenditure on public passenger transport services

88.—(1) Any power conferred on any authority responsible Expenditure for expenditure on public passenger transport services to enter on public into agreements providing for service subsidies (however framed, passenger and whether arising under this Act or under any other enact- services. ment) shall be subject to sections 89 to 92 of this Act.

(2) It shall be the duty—

    (*a*) of all such authorities, in exercising and performing their functions with respect to securing the provision of public passenger transport services ; and

    (*b*) of all authorities who are—

        (i) local education authorities in England and Wales or education authorities in Scotland ; or

        (ii) local authorities exercising, in England and Wales, social services functions or, in Scotland, social work functions ;

    in relation to any expenditure on transport for the purposes of or in connection with the exercise and performance of their functions as local education authorities or education authorities or (as the case may be) of their social services or social work functions ;

to co-operate with one another so as to secure, in the interests of the ratepayers of their areas, the best value for money from their expenditure on public passenger transport, taken as a whole.

(3) In subsection (2)(*b*)(ii) above " local authority " means—

    (*a*) in relation to England and Wales, an authority who are a local authority for the purposes of the Local Auth- 1970 c. 42. ority Social Services Act 1970 ; and

    (*b*) in relation to Scotland, an authority who are a local authority for the purposes of the Social Work (Scotland) 1968 c. 49. Act 1968.

(4) It shall be the duty of all authorities mentioned in sub-section (2) above to afford to one another such information as may be reasonably required for the purpose of the co-operation required of them under that subsection.

(5) Where, as a result of any such co-operation, any such authority—

    (*a*) incur expenditure which they would not otherwise have incurred ; or

    (*b*) receive less revenue than they would otherwise have done ;

that authority may, by notice to the other authority or authorities concerned, require that other authority or (as the case may be) those other authorities to reimburse the amount of that expenditure or of that reduction in revenue.

(6) If—

(*a*) any amount in respect of which, in accordance with a notice under subsection (5) above, any such authority or authorities are required to reimburse another such authority; or

(*b*) where two or more such authorities are required by any such notice to reimburse another such authority, the share of that amount payable by each authority concerned;

is not determined by agreement between both or all the authorities concerned within six months of the receipt of the notice or such longer period as may be agreed between them, that amount and (where paragraph (*b*) above applies) the share payable by each authority concerned shall be determined by an arbitrator or, in Scotland, by an arbiter.

(7) Any such arbitrator or (as the case may be) arbiter shall be appointed either by agreement between the authorities concerned or, in default of such agreement, by the President of the Chartered Institute of Public Finance and Accountancy.

(8) References in this Part of this Act to authorities responsible for expenditure on public passenger transport services are references to—

(*a*) Passenger Transport Executives;

(*b*) non-metropolitan county and district councils in England and Wales; and

(*c*) regional and islands councils in Scotland;

and in sections 89 to 92 of this Act include references to London Regional Transport in relation to any exercise of their power under section 3(2) of the London Regional Transport Act 1984 (contracting-out powers) which by virtue of section 65(3) of this Act is subject to those sections.

1984 c. 32.

Obligation to invite tenders for subsidised services.

89.—(1) Subject to sections 90 and 91 of this Act, an authority responsible for expenditure on public passenger transport services may not enter into an agreement providing for service subsidies under which a local service is to be provided except by accepting a tender invited in pursuance of this section.

(2) Where any such authority propose to secure the provision of any local service by entering into any such agreement, the authority shall invite tenders for the provision of that service for

such period and on such basis as may be specified in the invitation to tender.

(3) An invitation to tender under this section may not include conditions with respect to the terms of employment of persons to be employed in providing any service to which the invitation to tender relates.

(4) Subject to subsection (5) below, any such invitation—

    (a) must be issued generally, in such manner as the authority issuing the invitation consider appropriate for bringing it to the attention of persons who may be interested ; and

    (b) must also be issued individually to all persons who have given to that authority a written notice indicating that they wish to receive invitations to tender for the provision of local services for that authority's area or (as the case may be) for the provision of such services of any description to which the invitation relates.

(5) Any such notice shall specify the address to which any such invitation is to be directed, and it shall be sufficient for the purposes of subsection (4)(b) above if the authority send the invitation to the person giving any such notice at the address so specified.

(6) An authority issuing an invitation to tender under this section shall not accept any tender submitted by a person who is not the holder of either—

    (a) a PSV operator's licence, not being—

        (i) a licence which is for the time being of no effect by reason of its suspension ; or

        (ii) a licence to which any condition is attached under section 26 of this Act prohibiting the holder from using vehicles under the licence to provide local services of all descriptions or (as the case may be) of any description to which the invitation relates ; or

    (b) a permit under section 22 of this Act.

(7) The authority issuing any invitation to tender under this section shall determine—

    (a) whether to accept a tender submitted in response to the invitation ; or

    (b) which (if any) of several such tenders to accept ;

solely by reference to what in their view is the most effective and economic application of the funds at their disposal for the payment of service subsidies.

(8) Subsection (7) above shall not be taken as requiring the authority to limit their consideration, in the case of any such invitation to tender, to the application of those funds for the purpose of securing the provision of the particular service to which that invitation to tender relates; and accordingly the authority may (in particular) take into account in making, in relation to any such invitation to tender, any determination to which that subsection applies—

(a) costs and benefits in relation to any proposed expenditure by that or any other authority for the purpose of securing the provision of any other public passenger transport service;

(b) costs and benefits in relation to any proposed expenditure on transport for the purposes of or in connection with the exercise and performance by that or any other authority of any functions of a description mentioned in section 88(2)(b) of this Act; and

(c) any matter appearing to the authority to be relevant to determining whether the particular service to which that invitation to tender relates, and any other relevant service, would be effectively provided by any person who has submitted a tender in response to that invitation to tender.

For the purposes of paragraph (c) above, a service other than the particular service there mentioned is relevant if the authority propose to incur expenditure for the purpose of securing its provision and any tender or proposal for the provision of that service by any such person is also under consideration by the authority.

Provisions supplementary to section 89.

90.—(1) The period specified in any invitation to tender issued under section 89 of this Act as the period for which a service to which the invitation relates is to be provided shall not exceed five years beginning with the date on which any agreement entered into by accepting a tender submitted in response to the invitation is concluded.

(2) Such information as may be prescribed with respect to any tenders submitted in response to any such invitation to tender shall be published by the authority issuing the invitation in such manner as may be prescribed.

(3) On entering into an agreement by accepting any such tender that authority shall publish in such manner as may be prescribed their reasons for considering that the payment of service subsidies to secure the service in question in accordance with the terms of that tender is conducive to achieving the most effective and economic application of the funds at their disposal for the payment of such subsidies.

(4) Regulations may provide for treating a specification of
terms of service, in such form as may be prescribed—

> (a) prepared, with reference to any invitation to tender
> issued under section 89 of this Act by any authority
> responsible for expenditure on public passenger trans-
> port services, by the authority issuing the invitation
> with respect to the provision of that service by a
> company to be formed in pursuance of any requirement
> under Part IV of this Act to carry on any business
> which includes any current activities of that authority ;
> and
>
> (b) ratified by that company after its formation within such
> period and in such manner as may be prescribed ;

as if it were a tender submitted in response to that invitation by
that company within any period allowed for the submission of
tenders in accordance with that invitation.

(5) The reference in subsection (1)(a) above to any current
activities of an authority responsible for expenditure on public
passenger transport services is a reference to any activities which
at the time when the specification of terms of service is pre-
pared are currently carried on by or on behalf of that authority, or by any body of which that authority is a member or
to which it appoints any members.

91.—(1) Regulations may provide for excluding from section Exceptions
89(1) of this Act agreements of any description specified in the from section
regulations ; and any such description may be framed by ref- 89.
erence to—

> (a) the description of service to which the agreement re-
> lates ;
>
> (b) the description of persons proposing to operate the
> service ;
>
> (c) the period for which the service is to be provided under
> the agreement ;
>
> (d) the aggregate amount of the service subsidies provided
> for under the agreement ; or
>
> (e) any other relevant circumstances.

(2) Section 89(1) of this Act shall not apply in any case where
it appears to an authority responsible for expenditure on public
passenger transport services that action is urgently required for
the purpose of—

> (a) maintaining an existing service ;
>
> (b) securing the provision of a service in place of a service
> which has ceased to operate ; or
>
> (c) securing the provision of a service to meet any public
> transport requirement which has arisen unexpectedly
> and ought in the opinion of the authority to be met
> without delay ;

and that it is necessary for that purpose to enter into an agreement providing for service subsidies in order to secure that service.

(3) Where by virtue of subsection (2) above any such authority enter into an agreement to which section 89(1) of this Act does not apply, the authority shall as soon as possible invite tenders for the provision of the service which is the subject of that agreement for such period and on such basis as may be specified in the invitation to tender ; and sections 89(3) to (8) and 90 of this Act shall apply in any such case as if the invitation had been issued under section 89(2).

(4) Any agreement entered into by virtue of subsection (2) above shall be made so as to remain in force no later than the end of the period of three months beginning with the day immediately following the end of the period allowed for the submission of tenders in accordance with the invitation to tender issued under subsection (3) above.

(5) Subject to the following provisions of this section, where—

(a) an invitation to tender for the provision of any service is issued under section 89(2) of this Act or subsection (3) above ; and

(b) no tender, or no tender which the authority issuing the invitation consider acceptable, is submitted in response to that invitation ;

any power of that authority to enter into an agreement providing for service subsidies in order to secure that service shall cease to be subject to section 89(1) of this Act.

(6) Any agreement which by virtue of subsection (5) above is entered into by an authority responsible for expenditure on public passenger transport services otherwise than by acceptance of a tender invited in pursuance of section 89 or subsection (3) above shall be made so as to remain in force no later than the end of the period specified in pursuance of section 90(1) of this Act in the invitation to tender mentioned in subsection (5)(a) above.

(7) On entering into any such agreement an authority shall publish in such manner as may be prescribed either—

(a) a statement that no tender was submitted in response to that invitation to tender ; or

(b) a statement of their reasons for considering that no tender so submitted was acceptable ;

as the case may require.

92.—(1) An authority responsible for expenditure on public passenger transport services shall, in the exercise and perform-ance of their functions in relation to agreements providing for service subsidies, so conduct themselves as not to inhibit compe-tition between persons providing or seeking to provide public passenger transport services in their area.

PART V
General
provisions
with respect
to the exercise
of service
subsidy
functions.

(2) Regulations under this section—

(a) may make further provision for regulating the exercise and performance by authorities responsible for expendi-ture on public passenger transport services of their functions in relation to agreements providing for ser-vice subsidies ; and

(b) may make provision for limiting to an amount specified in the regulations the aggregate amount of the service subsidies any such authority may agree to pay under any one such agreement ; and

(c) may make provision for exceptions from section 89(4) of this Act in such cases as may be prescribed.

(3) The provisions of sections 89 to 91 of this Act shall be subject to this section and any provision made by regulations under this section.

Travel concession schemes

93.—(1) Any local authority, or any two or more local auth-orities acting jointly, may establish a travel concession scheme for the provision of travel concessions on journeys on public passenger transport services—

(a) between places in the principal area covered by the scheme ;

(b) between such places and places outside but in the vicinity of that area ; or

(c) between places outside but in the vicinity of that area ;

by operators of such services participating in the scheme.

(2) For the purposes of this section, the principal area covered by a scheme under this section is—

(a) the area of the local authority concerned or, where two or more such authorities are concerned, the area com-prising the areas of both or all those authorities ; or

(b) if an area comprised within the area which would be the principal area under paragraph (a) above is specified in the scheme as being the principal area to which the scheme applies, the area so specified.

(3) Any travel concession scheme established under this section shall define—

(*a*) the travel concessions which are for the time being to be provided by operators participating in the scheme ;

(*b*) the description of persons eligible in accordance with subsection (7) below to receive travel concessions under any such scheme who are for the time being to qualify for travel concessions provided under the scheme ; and

(*c*) the dates in any year currently adopted as the dates on which operators may be admitted to participate in the scheme under section 96 of this Act (referred to below in this section as the standard admission dates) ;

and may include particulars of any other arrangements for the time being adopted by the authority or authorities concerned in establishing the scheme with respect to the operation, scope and application of the scheme.

(4) Any such scheme may define the standard admission dates by specifying particular dates, or by referring to dates of any specified description or separated by intervals of any specified length ; but those dates, however determined, must not be separated by intervals of a length exceeding such period as may be prescribed.

(5) Arrangements adopted by the authority or authorities concerned in establishing any such scheme with respect to the operation, scope and application of the scheme (including the matters specifically mentioned in paragraphs (*a*) to (*c*) of sub-section (3) above) may differ for different descriptions of concessions or services to which the scheme applies.

(6) Subject to section 94 of this Act, where an operator participating in any such scheme in respect of any services operated by him provides travel concessions in accordance with the scheme for persons travelling on those services, the authority responsible for administration of the scheme or (as the case may be) the authorities so responsible in such proportions respectively as they may agree among themselves shall reimburse that operator for providing those concessions.

(7) The persons eligible to receive travel concessions under any such scheme are—

(*a*) men over the age of sixty-five years and women over the age of sixty years ;

(*b*) persons whose age does not exceed sixteen years ;

(*c*) persons whose age exceeds sixteen years but does not exceed eighteen years and who are undergoing full-time education ;

(*d*) blind persons, that is to say, persons so blind as to be unable to perform any work for which sight is essential ;

(*e*) persons suffering from any disability or injury which, in the opinion of the authority or any of the authorities responsible for administration of the scheme, seriously impairs their ability to walk ; and

(*f*) such other classes of persons as the Secretary of State may by order specify.

(8) In this section " local authority "—

(*a*) means the council of a county or district in England and Wales or a regional or islands council in Scotland ; and

(*b*) includes also, in relation to England and Wales, a metropolitan county passenger transport authority.

(9) Unless the context otherwise requires, references in this section and in the provisions of this Part of this Act relating to schemes under this section to the authority or authorities responsible for administration of a scheme under this section are references—

(*a*) except in a case to which paragraph (*b*) below applies, to the authority concerned in establishing the scheme or, where two or more authorities are so concerned, to both or all those authorities acting jointly ; or

(*b*) where the authority or one of the authorities concerned in establishing the scheme are a Passenger Transport Authority for a passenger transport area in England and Wales, to the Passenger Transport Executive for that Authority's area or (as the case may require) to that Executive and the other authority or authorities so concerned acting jointly.

(10) Where a Passenger Transport Authority have established a scheme under this section, whether alone or jointly with any other authority or authorities, they shall notify the Passenger Transport Executive for their area of any proposal to vary the scheme, giving particulars of the proposed variation.

94.—(1) Regulations under this section may make provision with respect to any of the following matters

(*a*) the factors to be taken into account by the authority or authorities responsible for administration of a travel concession scheme under section 93 of this Act in determining the aggregate amount that may be made available for the purpose of reimbursing operators participating in the scheme for providing travel concessions during any period ;

(*b*) the determination by the authority or authorities so responsible of the amounts to be paid to individual operators participating in the scheme, or to any class of such operators, by way of reimbursement for providing such concessions ;

(c) the manner of making any payments due to operators by way of such reimbursement ;

(d) the provisions or descriptions of provisions that are to be or (as the case may be) may or may not be included in arrangements agreed with operators or adopted by the authority or authorities so responsible with respect to participation of operators in the scheme ; and

(e) the terms on which and the extent to which the authority or authorities so responsible may employ any person as their agent for the purposes of the administration of the scheme and the descriptions of persons who may be so employed.

(2) Subject to any provision of regulations made by virtue of subsection (1)(d) above and to the following provisions of this section, the arrangements with respect to participation of operators in any such scheme shall be such as may from time to time be agreed between the authority or authorities responsible for administration of the scheme and individual operators.

(3) Subject to—

(a) any provision of regulations under subsection (1) above ;

(b) any modifications that may by virtue of any provision of regulations made by virtue of paragraph (d) of that subsection or in accordance with section 96 of this Act be agreed between the authority or authorities responsible for administration of any such scheme and any individual operator ; and

(c) any modifications applied in the case of any individual operator by a direction given under section 98 of this Act ;

the arrangements with respect to reimbursement and terms of withdrawal from participation in the scheme applicable to operators of eligible services participating in the scheme shall be such as the authority or authorities responsible for administration may from time to time adopt and must be the same in the case of all such operators.

(4) For the purposes of the provisions of this Part of this Act relating to schemes under section 93 of this Act, a service is an eligible service if it is a service qualifying for fuel duty grant.

(5) The arrangements currently adopted by the authority or authorities responsible for administration of any such scheme with respect to reimbursement of operators of eligible services

participating in the scheme are referred to below in this Part of this Act, in relation to that scheme, as the current reimbursement arrangements for eligible service operators participating in the scheme.

(6) In relation to operators participating in any such scheme, references in this section to arrangements with respect to reimbursement are references to conditions of entitlement of such operators to, and the method of determination and manner of payment of, reimbursement in respect of travel concessions provided under the scheme.

95.—(1) On or before the date on which a scheme under section 93 of this Act comes into operation or, where it comes into operation on different dates with respect to different concessions to be provided under the scheme, on or before the first of those dates—

(a) the authority or authorities concerned in establishing it shall publish particulars of the scheme ; and

(b) the authority or authorities responsible for administration of the scheme shall publish particulars of the current reimbursement arrangements for eligible service operators participating in the scheme as they are to apply on initial establishment of the scheme ;

in such manner, in either case, as the authority or authorities concerned think fit.

(2) Particulars of any subsequent variations shall be published—

(a) in the case of variations of the scheme, by the authority or authorities concerned in establishing the scheme ; and

(b) in the case of variations of the arrangements, by the authority or authorities responsible for administration of the scheme.

(3) Following publication under subsection (1)(a) or (as the case may be) under subsection (1)(b) above of particulars of any scheme or arrangements—

(a) copies of the scheme or (as the case may be) of the arrangements (with any subsequent variations) shall be made available at the principal office of the authority or (as the case may be) of each authority concerned ; and

(b) a copy shall be supplied to any person on request (whether at that office or by post) either free of charge or at a charge representing the cost of providing the copy.

PART V

(4) Where the authority or any of the authorities concerned in establishing a scheme under section 93 of this Act are a Passenger Transport Authority, they shall notify the Passenger Transport Executive for their area of any proposal to publish particulars of the scheme in advance of its coming into operation, giving the proposed date of publication.

Right of eligible service operators to participate in travel concession schemes.

96.—(1) Subject to the following provisions of this section, where any operator or prospective operator of an eligible service which runs or will run between places within the limits covered by any scheme under section 93 of this Act applies to the authority or authorities responsible for administration of that scheme to be admitted to participate in it in respect of that service, the authority or authorities in question shall be obliged to admit that operator to participation in the scheme in respect of that service as from any standard admission date under the scheme not later than the one next following—

(a) the end of such period as may be prescribed beginning with the date of his application ; or

(b) the date on which the service begins ;

whichever last occurs.

(2) The Secretary of State may, on the application of the authority or authorities responsible for administration of any such scheme, exempt the authority or authorities in question from the obligation under subsection (1) above in relation to any service or description of services ; and the Secretary of State may at any time withdraw or vary any exemption granted under this subsection.

(3) An exemption may not be granted under subsection (2) above on the application of a Passenger Transport Executive, or on the joint application of authorities who include such an Executive, unless the application is made with the consent of the Passenger Transport Authority for that Executive's area.

(4) Subject to any regulations under section 94(1)(d) of this Act, where it appears to the authority or authorities responsible for administration of any such scheme, in the case of any operator or prospective operator of an eligible service who applies to be admitted to participate in the scheme in respect of that service, that fares currently charged or proposed to be charged by that operator for relevant journeys on that service include a special amenity element, the authority or authorities in question shall not be required by subsection (1) above to admit that operator to participation in the scheme in respect of that service unless that operator agrees to appropriate modifications of the current reimbursement arrangements for eligible service operators participating in the scheme.

(5) Subject to any such regulations, where it appears to the authority or authorities responsible for administration of any such scheme, in the case of any operator of an eligible service participating in the scheme, that fares currently charged by that operator for relevant journeys on that service include a special amenity element, the authority or authorities in question may by notice of not less than such period as may be prescribed exclude that operator from participation in the scheme in respect of that service unless before the end of that period that operator agrees to appropriate modifications of the current reimbursement arrangements for eligible service operators participating in the scheme.

PART V

(6) For the purposes of subsections (4) and (5) above fares for relevant journeys are to be regarded as including a special amenity element if they are significantly high in relation to the general level of fares for comparable journeys in the principal area covered by the scheme (within the meaning of section 93 of this Act).

(7) References in those subsections to appropriate modifications of the reimbursement arrangements there mentioned are references to such modifications of those arrangements as the authority or authorities concerned consider appropriate for providing reimbursement in respect of travel concessions provided for relevant journeys on the service in question by reference to the general level of fares mentioned in subsection (6) above instead of by reference to the actual fares charged (or proposed to be charged) for those journeys.

(8) For the purposes of this section " relevant journeys " are journeys on which travel concessions are to be provided under the scheme in question.

(9) For the purposes of this section and section 97 of this Act, references to a prospective operator of an eligible service are references to a person who has registered a local service under section 6 of this Act but is not yet operating that service.

97.—(1) Subject to subsection (8) below, where the arrangements currently adopted by the authority or authorities responsible for administration of a scheme under section 93 of this Act with respect to the terms on which operators of eligible services may withdraw from participation in the scheme require such an operator to give notice before withdrawing from the scheme in respect of any such service, any such operator shall be obliged to provide any travel concessions required by the scheme on journeys on any such service in respect of which he is participating in the scheme until he gives the required notice of withdrawal and the period of notice has expired.

Compulsory participation in travel concession schemes.

E

(2) Subject to the following provisions of this section, the authority or authorities responsible for administration of any such scheme may at any time by notice in writing served on any operator or prospective operator of an eligible service (including an operator already participating in the scheme) impose on him an obligation to provide travel concessions in accord-ance with the scheme on journeys on any such service operated by that operator to which the notice applies.

A notice under this subsection is referred to below in this Part of this Act as a participation notice.

(3) The power under subsection (2) above to serve a participa-tion notice shall not be exercisable in relation to any such scheme until after the date (or whichever last occurs of the respective dates) of first publication under section 95 of this Act of particulars of the scheme and of the current reimbursement arrangements for eligible service operators participating in the scheme as they are to apply on initial establishment of the scheme.

(4) An obligation imposed by a participation notice shall, subject to subsection (8) below and sections 98 and 99 of this Act, be effective in relation to any service to which the obliga-tion applies as from the appropriate commencement date for that service until the end of such period beginning with that date as may be specified in the participation notice.

(5) Subject to subsection (9) below, for the purposes of sub-section (4) above the appropriate commencement date for any service to which an obligation imposed by a participation notice applies is—

> (a) the date immediately following the end of such period of notice as may be specified in the participation notice ; or
>
> (b) the date when the service begins ;

whichever last occurs.

(6) Where it is proposed—

> (a) to vary a scheme under section 93 of this Act ; or
>
> (b) to vary the current reimbursement arrangements for eligible service operators participating in any such scheme ;

the authority or authorities responsible for administration of the scheme may, not less than such period before the variation is to take effect as may be prescribed, by notice served on any operator of any such service who is under an obligation under this section to provide travel concessions in accordance with the scheme, require him to indicate, within such period and in such manner as may be prescribed, whether or not he is willing to continue to participate in the scheme after the variation takes effect.

(7) Any notice under subsection (6) above shall give particulars of the proposed variation.

(8) Where in pursuance of subsection (6) above an operator indicates that he is not willing to continue to participate in the scheme after the variation takes effect, any obligation of that operator under this section to provide travel concessions in accordance with the scheme which was current at the date of the notice under that subsection and would still apart from this subsection be in force on the date when the variation takes effect shall cease on the latter date (without prejudice, however, to the service of a new participation notice).

(9) Where a notice is served on an operator under subsection (6) above the preceding provisions of this section shall apply, on and after the date when the variation in question takes effect, in relation to any obligation of that operator under subsection (2) above to provide travel concessions in accordance with the scheme in question which—

    (*a*) was current at the date of the notice ; and

    (*b*) does not cease (by virtue of subsection (8) above or otherwise) before the date when that variation takes effect ;

as if the latter date were the appropriate commencement date for the purposes of subsection (4) above for each service to which the obligation applies.

(10) The exercise of the power to serve a participation notice under this section on any person—

    (*a*) by a Passenger Transport Executive ; or

    (*b*) by authorities responsible for administration of a scheme under section 93 of this Act who include such an Executive ;

shall require the consent of the Passenger Transport Authority for the Executive's area.

98.—(1) The authority or authorities by whom a participation notice is served on any person shall send to that person, together with the notice, a copy of—

    (*a*) such particulars of the scheme to which the notice relates and of any variations of that scheme ; and

    (*b*) such particulars of the current reimbursement arrangements for eligible service operators participating in the scheme and of any variations of those arrangements ;

E 2

as have been published under section 95 of this Act before the date of the notice.

(2) Subject to the following provisions of this section, a person on whom a participation notice has been served may apply to the Secretary of State for cancellation or variation of that notice on either or both of the following grounds, that is to say—

(a) that there are special reasons why his participation in the scheme in question in respect of the service or any of the services to which the notice applies would be inappropriate ; and

(b) that any provision of the scheme or of any such arrangements as are mentioned in subsection (1)(b) above are inappropriate for application in relation to operators other than operators voluntarily participating in the scheme.

(3) Subject to subsection (4) below, an application under subsection (2) above may be made by notice in writing given to the Secretary of State before the end of the period of twenty-eight days beginning with the date of the participation notice.

(4) A person may not make such an application unless he has given notice in writing of his intention to do so to the authority or authorities by whom the participation notice was served—

(a) if a period allowed for that purpose is specified in the participation notice, before the end of that period ; or

(b) in any other case, at any time before the date of the notice given to the Secretary of State under subsection (3) above.

(5) Where on any such application the Secretary of State finds the ground mentioned in subsection (2)(a) above established, he may cancel the participation notice or (as the case may require) vary it by excluding from it any service operated by the applicant in respect of which he considers the applicant's participation in the scheme would be inappropriate.

(6) Where on any such application the Secretary of State finds the ground mentioned in subsection (2)(b) above established, he shall cancel the participation notice unless he considers that a direction under subsection (7) below would meet the case.

(7) Where on any such application the Secretary of State does not cancel the participation notice, he may direct that the current arrangements for reimbursement of eligible service operators participating in the scheme shall apply in the case of the applicant or (as the case may require) in the case of any

service operated by the applicant to which the participation notice applies with such modifications as may be specified in the direction.

(8) If the Secretary of State cancels a participation notice under subsection (6) above he shall give to the authority or authorities by whom the notice was served a notice in writing indicating in what respects the scheme or (as the case may be) the current reimbursement arrangements for eligible service operators participating in the scheme are inappropriate for application in relation to operators other than operators voluntarily participating in the scheme.

(9) Any obligation under section 97(2) of this Act which has come into effect before the determination of any application under this section with respect to the participation notice by which that obligation was imposed shall—

(a) cease to have effect, if the notice is cancelled ; or

(b) have effect, if the notice is varied, subject to a corresponding variation ;

on such date as may be specified by the Secretary of State in determining the application.

99.—(1) The authority or authorities responsible for administration of a scheme under section 93 of this Act may at any time by notice in writing served on any operator who is under an obligation under section 97(2) of this Act to provide travel concessions in accordance with the scheme on journeys on any eligible service operated by him release him from that obligation in respect of that service.

(2) Subject to the following provisions of this section, any such operator may at any time by notice in writing apply to the Secretary of State to be released from that obligation in respect of any such service on the ground that the authority or authorities responsible for administration of the scheme have failed to comply with their obligation under section 93(6) of this Act.

(3) An operator may not make such an application unless he has given notice in writing of his intention to do so to the authority or authorities responsible for administration of the scheme not less than twenty-eight days before the date of the application.

(4) A notice under subsection (2) or (3) above shall give particulars of any alleged failures of the authority or authorities in question to comply with their obligation under section 93(6) of which the operator complains.

(5) On any such application the Secretary of State may, if he finds the applicant's ground of complaint established, determine

PART V

that the applicant's obligation under section 97(2) shall cease on such date as may be specified in the determination.

Provisions
Supplemen-
tary to sections
96 to 99

100.—(1) Regulations under this section may make provision as to—

(a) the maximum or (as the case may be) minimum period that may for the purposes of any provision of section 97 or 98 of this Act be specified in a participation notice ;

(b) the form and contents of participation notices and other notices required for any purposes of sections 96 to 99 of this Act ; and

(c) the manner in which any such notice is to be served.

(2) Where the Secretary of State cancels or varies a participation notice under section 98 of this Act after the obligation imposed by that notice has come into effect he may award compensation to the applicant under subsection (4) below if it appears to him that the applicant has suffered—

(a) in a case where the notice is cancelled, any loss attributable to his participation in the scheme in question ; or

(b) in a case where the notice is varied by excluding from it any service operated by the applicant, any loss attributable to his participation in that scheme in respect of that service.

(3) Where on determining an application under section 99 of this Act the Secretary of State finds that the authority or authorities responsible for administration of the scheme in question have failed to comply with their obligation under section 93(6) of this Act, he may award compensation to the applicant under subsection (4) below if it appears to him that the applicant has suffered any loss attributable to that failure.

(4) In any case to which subsection (2) or (3) above applies the Secretary of State may by notice in writing require the authority responsible for administration of the scheme in question or (as the case may be) the authorities so responsible in such proportions as may be specified in the notice to pay to the applicant such an amount by way of compensation in respect of the loss there mentioned as may be so specified.

(5) The Secretary of State may if he thinks fit appoint a person to determine an application under section 98 or 99 of this Act on his behalf ; and references in those sections and in subsections (2) to (4) above to the Secretary of State shall be read as including references to a person so appointed.

(6) Regulations under this section may prescribe the procedure to be followed in connection with applications under sections 98 and 99 of this Act and may in particular (but without prejudice to the generality of that) include provision—

> (a) as to the conduct of any proceedings held in connection with any such application ; and

> (b) enabling the Secretary of State to require either the applicant or the authority or authorities responsible for administration of the scheme in question, or both or all of them, to pay such sum as the Secretary of State may determine towards any expenses incurred by him in connection with the determination of the application.

(7) Where a requirement under subsection (4) above is imposed on more than one authority, the liability of the authorities concerned to the applicant—

> (a) shall extend to the whole of the amount specified in the notice imposing the requirement ; and

> (b) shall be both joint and several ;

but if any such authority make any payment, in or towards the discharge of that liability, of an amount exceeding the amount representing any proportion specified in the notice as that authority's share, that authority shall be entitled to recover an appropriate contribution (determined by reference to the proportions specified in that notice) from the other authority or authorities concerned.

(8) Any sums paid to the Secretary of State by virtue of subsection (6)(*b*) above shall be paid into the Consolidated Fund.

101.—(1) If during any period an operator of any service who is under an obligation under section 97 of this Act to provide travel concessions in accordance with a scheme under section 93 of this Act for persons travelling on that service systematically fails to comply with that obligation he shall be liable on summary conviction to a fine not exceeding level 3 on the standard scale.

Enforcement of participation in travel concession schemes.

(2) Where an offence under this section committed by a body corporate is proved to have been committed with the consent or connivance of, or to have been attributable to any neglect on the part of, any director, manager, secretary or other similar officer of the body corporate or a person who was purporting to act in any such capacity, he as well as the body corporate shall be guilty of that offence and shall be liable to be proceeded against and punished accordingly.

(3) Where the affairs of a body corporate are managed by its members, subsection (2) above shall apply in relation to the acts and defaults of a member in connection with his functions of management as if he were a director of the body corporate.

(4) Proceedings for an offence under this section shall not, in England and Wales, be instituted except by the authority, or any one of the authorities, responsible for administration of the scheme in question or by or with the consent of the Director of Public Prosecutions (and any such authority who would not apart from this subsection have power to bring such proceedings shall accordingly have that power).

Application of Passenger Transport Executive's financial plan to expenditure on travel concessions under schemes.
1983 c. 10.

102.—(1) In section 3 of the Transport Act 1983 (preparation and submission of financial plans by Passenger Transport Executive)—

(a) in subsection (1), the word " and " immediately following paragraph (a) shall be omitted, and after paragraph (b) there shall be added the following words—

" and

(c) the general level and structure of travel concessions (meaning reductions or waivers of fares) to be provided in the relevant period under any scheme established by the Authority under section 93 of the Transport Act 1985 (whether alone or jointly with any local authority within the meaning of that section)." ;

(b) in subsection (3), after " 1968 " there shall be inserted the words " or for carrying out their functions with respect to the administration of any such scheme as is mentioned in subsection (1)(c) above " ; and

(c) in subsection (4), the word " and " immediately following paragraph (b) shall be omitted, and after paragraph (c) there shall be added the following words—

" and

(d) the cost to the Executive of reimbursing persons providing travel concessions under any such scheme as is mentioned in subsection (1)(c) above.".

(2) In section 4 of that Act—

(a) in subsection (2)(c), at the end there shall be added the words " or (as the case may be) as to the cost of requiring under any such scheme as is mentioned in section 3(1)(c) above the provision of travel concessions at a level higher than, or differently structured from, the level and structure of such concessions for which that scheme currently provides." ; and

(*b*) in subsection (3)(*a*), for " (*c*) " there shall be substituted " (*d*) ".

Part V

Travel concessions apart from schemes

103.—(1) The payments provided for under an agreement providing for service subsidies entered into by an authority responsible for expenditure on public passenger transport services may not include payments in respect of the provision of travel concessions except as provided below in this section.

Subsidies for travel concessions.

(2) Subject to subsection (3) below, provision may be included in any such agreement for the making of payments by the authority in question to the person providing the service to which the agreement relates in respect of the provision of travel concessions on journeys on that service or any part of it for any description of persons eligible in accordance with section 93(7) of this Act to receive travel concessions under a travel concession scheme under that section.

(3) Subsection (2) above only applies where the concessions in question are not available, or not available to that description of persons, under any such scheme administered by the authority concerned or by that authority acting jointly with any other authority or authorities.

104.—(1) A Passenger Transport Executive may not in exercise of their powers under section 10(1)(xiii) of the 1968 Act (power of Passenger Transport Executive to charge for services and waive their charges, etc.) provide travel concessions for persons travelling on any public passenger transport service provided by the Executive other than persons of any description eligible in accordance with section 93(7) of this Act to receive travel concessions under a travel concession scheme established under that section, except where those concessions are provided under any agreement or arrangements under which the whole of the cost of providing those concessions is to be met by a person other than that Executive or the Passenger Transport Authority for that Executive's area.

Travel concessions on services provided by Passenger Transport Executives.

(2) The approval of the Passenger Transport Authority for a passenger transport area under section 15(2) of the 1968 Act (approval of Passenger Transport Authority required for alterations by Executive in general level of charges and for reduction or waiver of charges by Executive) shall not be required for travel concessions granted by the Passenger Transport Executive for that area for persons travelling on any public passenger

PART V

transport service provided by the Executive if those concessions are granted—

    (a) in accordance with any scheme established under section 93 of this Act by any authority other than the Passenger Transport Authority for that Executive's area or (as the case may be) by authorities who do not include that Passenger Transport Authority ; or

    (b) where that Executive's area is in England and Wales, in pursuance of arrangements made with that Executive by any local authority within the meaning of the National Assistance Act 1948 in exercise of their powers under section 29 of that Act (welfare arrangements for handicapped persons) ;

1948 c. 29.

or correspond to travel concessions under any scheme established under section 93 of this Act by the Passenger Transport Authority for that Executive's area or (as the case may be) by authorities who include that Passenger Transport Authority.

(3) For the purposes of subsection (2) above, travel concessions granted by the Executive for a passenger transport area on any such service correspond to travel concessions under any such scheme if they are—

    (a) of the same value ;

    (b) available subject to the same terms, limitations or conditions ; and

    (c) available to persons of the same description ;

as the travel concessions provided under that scheme.

Travel concessions on services provided by local authorities.

105.—(1) Where the council of any county or district in England and Wales or of any region or islands area in Scotland are operating any public passenger transport service, they shall have power to provide travel concessions for persons travelling on that service of any description eligible in accordance with section 93(7) of this Act to receive travel concessions under a travel concession scheme established under that section.

(2) In respect of travel concessions provided under this section, any such council may, if they think fit, from time to time transfer to the credit of the account of their transport undertaking sums from the general rate fund or, where that council is the council of any region or islands area in Scotland, from the general fund (within the meaning of section 93 of the Local Government (Scotland) Act 1973).

1973 c. 65.

(3) Sums so transferred must not exceed the cost to the council concerned of providing the concessions or so much of that cost as would not apart from subsection (2) above fall to be met out of the fund there mentioned.

Grants for transport facilities and services

106.—(1) Any authority to whom this section applies, or any Grants for two or more such authorities acting jointly, may make, in such transport cases and subject to such terms and conditions as they think fit, facilities and grants to any other person towards expenditure incurred or to be services. incurred by that person in providing, maintaining or improving

> (a) any vehicle, equipment or other facilities provided wholly or mainly for the purpose of facilitating travel by members of the public who are disabled ; or
>
> (b) any equipment or other facilities specially designed or adapted for that purpose which are incorporated in any vehicle, equipment or other facilities not provided wholly or mainly for that purpose.

(2) Subject to subsection (3) below, any such authority, or any two or more such authorities acting jointly, may make, in such cases and subject to such terms and conditions as they think fit, grants to any person providing public passenger transport services towards expenditure incurred or to be incurred by that person for the purpose of—

> (a) maintaining or improving facilities for public passenger transport, other than facilities provided wholly or mainly for use for the purpose of or in connection with excepted services ; or
>
> (b) facilitating or improving the operation of public passenger transport services, other than excepted services ;

in the area of that authority or (as the case may be) in the area comprising the areas of both or all those authorities.

In this subsection " excepted services " means services for the carriage of passengers by road which require a PSV operator's licence (within the meaning of Part IV of this Act).

(3) Subsection (2) above shall not apply in relation to expenditure appearing to the authority or authorities in question to be of a capital nature.

(4) This section applies to the following authorities—

> (a) any Passenger Transport Authority or Passenger Transport Executive ;
>
> (b) the council of any county or district in England and Wales ;
>
> (c) the council of a London borough or the Common Council of the City of London ; or
>
> (d) any regional or islands council in Scotland.

Grants for services for disabled people in London

107.—(1) London Regional Transport may make, in such Grants by cases and subject to such terms and conditions as they think fit, London Regional Transport.

PART V   grants to any voluntary organisation for the purpose of meeting (in whole or in part) any expenditure incurred or to be incurred by that organisation for the purpose of the provision of transport services provided by that organisation solely to meet the needs of disabled members of the public resident in London.

(2) In subsection (1) above " voluntary organisation " means a body the activities of which are carried on otherwise than for profit, but does not include any public or local authority.

Grants for services in rural areas

Grants for establishment, etc., of rural passenger services in Wales and Scotland.

108.—(1) Subject to the following provisions of this section, the Secretary of State may, with the approval of the Treasury, make in such cases as he thinks fit a grant to any person for the purpose of securing the establishment, continuance or improvement of any public passenger transport service which in the opinion of the Secretary of State is or will be for the benefit of persons residing in any rural area in Wales or Scotland.

(2) In the case of any grant under this section for the purpose of securing the continuance of an existing service—

(*a*) the service must be one which was established with the assistance of a grant under this section ; and

(*b*) the grant must be for securing its continuance during such period from the time when it was first operated as appears to the Secretary of State to be appropriate in the case of that service.

(3) In the case of any grant under this section for the purpose of securing the improvement of an existing service the improvement in view must be one which appears to the Secretary of State to involve an innovative approach to the use of vehicles, equipment or other facilities in providing the service.

(4) Grants under this section shall be of such amount and subject to such conditions (including conditions requiring their repayment in specified circumstances) as the Secretary of State may, with the approval of the Treasury, determine, either generally or in relation to any particular cases or classes of case.

Transitional rural bus grants.

109.—(1) Subject to the following provisions of this section, the Secretary of State may, with the approval of the Treasury, make in such cases as he thinks fit a grant to any person in respect of qualifying mileage run at any time during the period of four years beginning with the date on which this section comes into force by vehicles used by that person in operating a service which at the time in question is a service eligible for grant under this section.

(2) A service is eligible for grant under this section at any
time when—

(a) it is a service qualifying for fuel duty grant ;

(b) it is being operated wholly or partly within a rural area
in Great Britain (outside London) ; and

(c) it meets such other requirements as the Secretary of
State thinks fit to impose ;

and in subsection (1) above " qualifying mileage " means, in
relation to any vehicle, mileage run by that vehicle within any
such rural area.

(3) Grants under this section shall be of such amount and
subject to such conditions (including conditions requiring their
repayment in specified circumstances) as the Secretary of State
may, with the approval of the Treasury, determine, either generally or in relation to any particular cases or classes of case.

Miscellaneous and supplementary

110.—(1) In section 92(1) of the Finance Act 1965 (grants to Grants
operators of bus services towards duty charged on bus fuel)— towards duty
charged on
(a) the words " any bus service " shall be omitted ; and bus fuel.

(b) there shall be inserted at the end the words— 1965 c. 25.

> " a bus service which is of a description specified
> for the purposes of this section and which meets any
> conditions which may be specified in relation to that
> description of service.".

(2) For subsection (8) of that section there shall be substituted the following subsections—

> " (8) In this section—

> " bus service " means a local service within the meaning
> of the Transport Act 1985 other than an excur-
> sion or tour within the meaning of that Act, being
> a service which is either—

>> (a) registered under Part I of that Act ; or

>> (b) provided under a London local service
>> licence granted under Part II of that Act or
>> exempt by virtue of section 36 of that Act
>> (London bus services under control of London
>> Regional Transport) from the requirement of
>> a London local service licence ;

> " operator " has the same meaning, in relation to a bus
> service, as in that Act ; and

> " specified " means specified in regulations made by the
> Secretary of State by statutory instrument.

PART V

(8A) Any statutory instrument containing regulations made under this section shall be subject to annulment in pursuance of a resolution of either House of Parliament."

Unregistered and unreliable local services: reduction of fuel duty grant.

111.—(1) Where the traffic commissioner for any traffic area is satisfied that the operator of a local service has, without reasonable excuse—

(a) failed to operate a local service registered under section 6 of this Act ; or

(b) to a significant extent operated a local service in contravention of that section ;

he may make a determination to that effect.

(2) Where a traffic commissioner makes a determination under subsection (1) above he shall notify the Secretary of State and the operator of the service in writing forthwith.

1965 c. 25.

(3) Where a determination has been made under subsection (1) above with respect to a local service there shall become due to the Secretary of State from the operator of the service an amount equal to twenty per cent. of any amount paid to him under section 92 of the Finance Act 1965 (grants to operators of bus services towards duty charged on bus fuel) in respect of all services operated during the period of three months ending with the day on which the traffic commissioner made his determination.

(4) The operator of any local service in respect of which a determination has been made under subsection (1) above may appeal to the Transport Tribunal against the determination.

(5) Any amount due to the Secretary of State under this section shall be recoverable as a debt due to the Crown ; and any amount repaid to, or recovered by, him under this section shall be paid into the Consolidated Fund.

Interpretation of Part V.

112.—(1) In this Part of this Act—

(a) references to authorities responsible for expenditure on public passenger transport services shall be read in accordance with section 88(8) of this Act ;

(b) references to service subsidies are references to the payments that fall to be made by any such authority under any agreement providing for service subsidies ;

(c) references to the current reimbursement arrangements for eligible service operators participating in any scheme under section 93 of this Act shall be read in accordance with section 94(5) of this Act ;

(d) references to a participation notice shall be read in accordance with section 97(2) of this Act;

(e) references to securing the provision of a service include references to securing the provision of a service by way of continuance of an existing service, and references in any other context to the provision of a service are to be read consistently with that; and

(f) " travel concession " means the reduction or waiver of a fare either absolutely or subject to terms, limitations or conditions.

(2) For the purposes of this Part of this Act, a service is a service qualifying for fuel duty grant at any time when fuel used in operating the service falls to be taken into account for the purpose of calculating grant payable to the operator of the service under section 92 of the Finance Act 1965 (grants to operators of bus services towards duty charged on bus fuel).

1965 c. 25.

PART VI

MISCELLANEOUS AND GENERAL

Exclusion of requirement to co-ordinate services of public sector transport undertakings

113.—(1) Section 24(3) of the 1968 Act (which imposes on the National Bus Company, the Railways Board and the Scottish Transport Group a duty to co-operate with one another for the purpose of co-ordinating the passenger transport services provided respectively by them or by their subsidiaries) shall cease to have effect.

Repeal of section 24(3) of the 1968 Act.

(2) In subsection (4) of that section, for the words " Subsections (2) and (3) " there shall be substituted the words " Subsection (2) ".

Competition law: bus services and bus stations

114.—(1) In section 11 of the Competition Act 1980 (references of public bodies and certain other persons subject to statutory controls to the Monopolies and Mergers Commission), in subsection (3) (which lists the persons who may be the subject of such a reference)—

Monopoly references with respect to bus services.

1980 c. 21.

(a) for paragraph (b) (any person not within paragraph (a) providing a bus service within the meaning of certain enactments) there shall be substituted the following paragraph—

PART VI

1966 c. 21
(N.I.).

1984 c. 32.

1973 c. 41.

" (b) any person (not falling within paragraph (a) above) who provides in Northern Ireland a bus service within the meaning of section 14 of the Finance Act (Northern Ireland) 1966 ; or " ; and

(b) in paragraph (bb), for the words " last-mentioned Act " there shall be substituted the words " London Regional Transport Act 1984 ".

(2) In Part I of Schedule 5 to the Fair Trading Act 1973 (which lists certain goods and services in respect of which references under section 14 of that Act to the Consumer Protection Advisory Committee or under section 50 or 51 of that Act to the Monopolies and Mergers Commission are excluded or, as the case may be, subject to restrictions not applicable in other cases)—

(a) for paragraph 4 (which at the passing of this Act refers to the carriage of passengers by road or rail) there shall be substituted the following paragraph—

" 4. The carriage of passengers by road in Northern Ireland " ; and

(b) in paragraph 5 (which at the passing of this Act refers to the carriage of goods by rail), after the word " goods " there shall be inserted the words " or passengers ".

(3) In paragraph 15(1) of Schedule 6 to the London Regional Transport Act 1984, paragraph (a) (amendment of section 11(3)

1980 c. 21.

(b) of the Competition Act 1980) shall be omitted.

Application of
Restrictive
Trade
Practices Act
1976 to
agreements
between road
passenger
transport
operators.
S.I. 1976/98.
1976 c. 34.

1981 c. 14.

115.—(1) In paragraph 4 of the Schedule to the Restrictive Trade Practices (Services) Order 1976 (which excepts certain agreements between road passenger transport operators from the agreements which by virtue of Article 3 of the Order are agreements to which the Restrictive Trade Practices Act 1976 applies)—

(a) in sub-paragraph (1) there shall be substituted for the words " of stage carriages or express carriages or both " the words " in Northern Ireland, or in Northern Ireland and the Republic of Ireland, of services, using one or more public service vehicles (within the meaning of the Public Passenger Vehicles Act 1981), for the carriage of passengers by road at separate fares." ; and

(b) sub-paragraph (2) shall be omitted.

(2) That Act shall have effect in relation to any agreement (within the meaning of that Act) made before this section comes into force as if the variation of that Order made by subsection

(1) above had been made by an order under section 11 of that
Act coming into force on the date on which this section comes
into force.

116.—(1) In subsection (3) of section 137 of the Fair Trading
Act 1973 (which defines " the supply of services " for the purposes of that Act and, by virtue of section 33(2) of the Competition Act 1980, for the purposes also of sections 2 to 24 of the
latter Act) there shall be inserted after paragraph (*c*)—

> " and
>
> > (*d*) includes the making of arrangements for the use by
> > public service vehicles (within the meaning of the
> > Public Passenger Vehicles Act 1981) of a parking place
> > which is used as a point at which passengers on services
> > provided by means of such vehicles may be taken up or
> > set down."

Use of bus
stations:
monopolies,
anti-
competitive
practices and
restrictive
trade
practices.
1973 c. 41.
1980 c. 21.
1981 c. 14.

(2) In section 20 of the Restrictive Trade Practices Act 1976
(interpretation of the Part of the Act dealing with services)
there shall be inserted after paragraph (*b*) in the definition of
" services "—

1976 c. 34.

> " and
>
> > (*c*) includes arrangements for the use by public service
> > vehicles (within the meaning of the Public Passenger
> > Vehicles Act 1981) of a parking place which is used as
> > a point at which passengers on services provided by
> > means of such vehicles may be taken up or set down."

(3) The Act of 1976 shall have effect in relation to any agreement (within the meaning of that Act) which—

> (*a*) was made before the date on which this section comes
> into force ; and
>
> (*b*) becomes subject to registration under that Act on that
> date by virtue of the effect which an order under section
> 11 of that Act has as a result of the coming into force
> of this section ;

as if it had become subject to registration by virtue of an order
under sections 11 coming into force on that date.

Reconstitution of the Transport Tribunal

117.—(1) The number of members of the Transport Tribunal
shall no longer be subject to any limit ; and the tribunal shall
no longer be required to sit in two divisions.

Reconstitution
of the
Transport
Tribunal.

(2) Schedule 4 to this Act shall have effect (in place of the
existing law) with respect to the constitution, powers and proceedings of the tribunal.

(3) The following panels, that is to say—

> (*a*) the special panel constituted in accordance with para-
> graph 6 of Schedule 10 to the 1962 Act (special panel
> for the purposes of the tribunal's jurisdiction under
> part V of the 1968 Act) ; and
>
> (*b*) any panel appointed under section 88(2)(*b*) of the 1968
> Act (panel of assessors for proceedings before the
> tribunal under Part V of that Act) ;

are abolished.

Road passenger transport services in place of railway services

Railways
Board's road
passenger
transport
services.

118.—(1) After section 4 of the 1962 Act (Railways Board's road services) there shall be inserted the following section—

" Railways
Board's
road
passenger
transport
services.

4A.—(1) Subject to this section, the Railways Board shall have power to secure the provision by other persons of services for the carriage of passengers by road where a railway service has been temporarily interrupted, or has been discontinued.

(2) The route (and stopping places) of any such service provided where a railway service has been discontinued need not correspond precisely with the route of the discontinued service (even where it is practicable to do so), so long as the service so provided broadly corresponds with the discontinued service, in terms of the localities it serves.

(3) Subsection (2) above is not to be taken as prejudicing the power of the Board under subsection (1) above to secure the provision of a service which deviates in any respect from the route of a railway service which has been interrupted or discontinued where it is not practicable for a service by road to correspond precisely to the railway service in question.

(4) Before entering into any agreement in pursuance of subsection (1) above for the provision by any other person of a service for the carriage of passengers by road in a case where a railway service has been discontinued, the Board shall invite other persons to submit tenders to provide that service for such period and on such basis as may be specified in the invitation to tender.

(5) Subsection (4) above shall not apply in relation to an agreement for the provision of such a service on a temporary basis in a case where a service for the carriage of passengers by road provided under

an agreement entered into by the Board in pursuance of subsection (1) above has been temporarily interrupted.

(6) Nothing in subsection (4) above shall be read as requiring the Board to accept any tender submitted in response to an invitation to tender issued under that subsection.

(7) The Railways Board may not under this section secure the provision by any person of a service for the carriage of passengers by road provided otherwise than by means of public service vehicles or licensed taxis.

(8) The Railways Board may not themselves directly provide services for the carriage of passengers by road.

(9) In this section—

(a) " licensed taxi " means—

(i) in England and Wales, a vehicle licensed under section 37 of the Town Police Clauses Act 1847 or section 6 of the Metropolitan Public Carriage Act 1869 or under any similar enactment; and

1847 c. 89.
1869 c. 115.

(ii) in Scotland, a taxi licensed under section 10 of the Civic Government (Scotland) Act 1982 ; and

1982 c. 45.

(b) " stopping place " means a point at which passengers are taken up or set down in the course of the service in question."

(2) Section 4 of the 1962 Act shall cease to apply in relation to services for the carriage of passengers by road ; and, accordingly, in that section—

(a) in subsection (1)—

(i) in paragraph (a), sub-paragraph (iii) and the words " and passengers " shall be omitted ; and

(ii) in paragraph (b) (Board's power to exercise powers conferred by the Railway Road Transport Acts of 1928), after the word " exercise " there shall be inserted the words " in relation to the carriage of goods by road " ;

(b) subsection (5) (nothing in that section to authorise Board to use hackney carriages plying or standing for hire) shall be omitted ; and

F 2

(*c*) in subsection (6) (exclusion of Board's power to provide
road transport services apart from that section) the
words " or passengers " shall be omitted.

Bus
substitution
services and
bus service
conditions.

119.—(1) This section applies where the Secretary of State
imposes a condition requiring the Railways Board to secure
the provision of an alternative service for the carriage of passengers by road—

    (*a*) under section 54(5) of the 1968 Act, in giving his con-
sent to the discontinuance by the Board of all railway
passenger services from any station or on any line
(referred to below in this section as a closure) ; or

    (*b*) under section 122 of this Act, in revoking any previous
condition to that effect (whether imposed as mentioned
in paragraph (*a*) above or imposed under section 122) ;

and any such service required by a condition so imposed is
referred to below in this Act as a bus substitution service.

(2) In any such case the Board shall secure the provision of
the bus substitution service in exercise of their powers under
section 4A of the 1962 Act (provision of road passenger transport services where a railway service has been interrupted or
discontinued) ; and subsection (2) of that section (which makes
provision with respect to the route and stopping places of any
service provided on discontinuance of a railway service) shall be
subject to the condition requiring the bus substitution service
and to any other condition imposed by the Secretary of State
in connection with the closure or (as the case may be) under
section 122 of this Act with respect to the operation of that
service.

(3) The Passenger Transport Executive for any passenger
transport area may enter into agreements with the Railways
Board under which the Executive make payments to the Board
in respect of the cost incurred by the Board in securing the
provision of any bus substitution service between places in the
Executive's area or between such places and places outside that
area but within the permitted distance for the purposes of section
10(1)(ii) of the 1968 Act as it applies to that Executive (that is to
say, twenty-five miles from the nearest point on the boundary of
that area).

(4) The Secretary of State may not vary or revoke any condition imposed by him as mentioned in subsection (1)(*a*) or (*b*)
above with respect to the provision or operation of a bus substitution service (referred to below in this Act as a bus service
condition) except as provided below in this section.

(5) A bus service condition requiring the Board to secure the provision of a bus substitution service may not be—

(*a*) revoked ; or

(*b*) varied so as to permit the Board to withdraw the service from any locality or point for the time being specified in the condition as a locality or point the service is required to serve ;

except in accordance with the procedure provided by sections 120 to 122 of this Act (which corresponds, with certain modifications, to the procedure applicable under section 56 of the 1962 Act in relation to a closure) ; but, subject to that, a bus service condition may at any time be varied or revoked by the Secretary of State.

120.—(1) Where the Railways Board propose— Notice of
withdrawal
(*a*) to seek revocation of a bus service condition requiring of bus
them to secure the provision of a bus substitution substitution
service ; or service.

(*b*) to seek variation of such a condition so as to permit them to withdraw any such service from any locality or point for the time being specified in the condition as a locality or point the service is required to serve ;

they shall, not less than six weeks before the date they propose for the withdrawal of the service or (as the case may be) for the withdrawal of the service from that locality or point (referred to below in this Act as the withdrawal of service) publish in two successive weeks in two local newspapers circulating in the area affected, and in such other manner as appears to them appropriate, a notice complying with subsection (2) below.

(2) The notice shall—

(*a*) give the date proposed by the Board for the withdrawal of service and particulars of the proposed withdrawal, of any alternative services which it appears to the Board will be available and of any proposals of the Board for securing the provision of alternative services or augmenting any available alternative services ; and

(*b*) state that objections to the revocation or (as the case may be) to the variation of the bus service condition may be lodged in accordance with this section within six weeks of a date specified in the notice.

(3) The date so specified shall be the date on which the notice is last published in a local newspaper as required by subsection (1) above.

(4) Copies of the notice published under subsection (1) above shall be sent to the appropriate Area Committee.

(5) Where the proposed withdrawal of service relates to a service or part of a service which is subsidised by the Passenger Transport Executive for any passenger transport area under any agreement made with the Railways Board by virtue of section 119(3) of this Act, the Board shall not publish a notice with respect to the proposed withdrawal under subsection (1) above without the consent of the Executive to its publication.

(6) If in any such case the Board publish such a notice before obtaining that consent, the notice shall be of no effect unless before the end of the period fixed by the notice for objecting to the revocation or variation of the relevant bus service condition either—

    (*a*) the Executive have informed the Board in writing that they consent to the publication ; or

    (*b*) the Secretary of State, on an application made for the purpose by the Board (whether before or after the publication of the notice) and after offering the Executive what the Secretary of State considers a reasonable opportunity to make any representations, has directed that the notice shall have effect notwithstanding that the Executive have not consented to its publication.

(7) Where in the case of any proposed withdrawal of service subsection (5) above does not apply but any locality or point affected by the proposed withdrawal is situated in a passenger transport area, the Railways Board shall send to the Passenger Transport Executive for that area a copy of the notice published by them under subsection (1) above.

Objections to withdrawal of bus substitution service.

121.—(1) Where a notice has been published by the Railways Board under section 120(1) of this Act, any user of any service affected and any body representing such users may within the period specified in the notice lodge with the appropriate Area Committee an objection in writing.

(2) Where such an objection is lodged the committee shall immediately inform the Secretary of State and the Board.

(3) A committee with whom an objection has been lodged under subsection (1) above shall consider the objection and any representations made by the Board and report to the Secretary of State as soon as possible on the hardship, if any, which they consider will be caused by the proposed withdrawal of service, and the report may contain proposals for alleviating that hardship.

(4) The Secretary of State may require a further report from any committee making a report to him under subsection (3) above.

(5) Copies of every report under subsection (3) or (4) above shall be sent to the Central Committee and to the Board.

(6) Where, in the case of any withdrawal of service to which section 120(5) or (7) of this Act applies, notice of the withdrawal has been published under subsection (1) of that section, the Executive concerned may, within the period specified in the notice for objecting to the withdrawal, lodge with the Secretary of State a statement in writing that they oppose the withdrawal and of their reasons for opposing it.

The fact that the Executive concerned gave their consent to the publication of the notice shall not affect their right under this subsection to oppose the withdrawal of service.

(7) Where the Executive for any passenger transport area lodge such a statement with the Secretary of State they shall send a copy of that statement to the Board.

(8) References above in this section to a notice published under section 120(1) of this Act do not include a notice which under subsection (6) of that section is of no effect.

122.—(1) Subject to subsection (2) below, where an objection to a proposed withdrawal of service is lodged under section 121 of this Act, the Secretary of State shall not revoke or (as the case may be) vary the bus service condition in question until he has received from the appropriate Area Committee the report required by subsection (3) of that section and any further report required by him under subsection (4) of that section.

(2) If in any case the Secretary of State considers that any such report has been unreasonably delayed he may, after consulting the committee concerned and making such enquiries as he thinks fit, revoke or vary the condition without waiting for the report.

(3) Where a statement opposing the proposed withdrawal is lodged by the Executive for a passenger transport area under section 121 of this Act, the Secretary of State shall have regard to that statement in determining whether to revoke or vary the bus service condition in question.

(4) In any case within subsection (1) or (3) above the Secretary of State shall have regard, in determining whether to revoke or vary the bus service condition in question, to any matters which

PART VI for the time being appear to him to be relevant, including any social or economic considerations, and shall not revoke or vary the condition in accordance with the Board's proposals—

    (a) unless he is satisfied that a reasonable opportunity has been afforded for the making to him of representations with respect to the proposed withdrawal of service by or on behalf of employees of the Board affected by that withdrawal ; or

    (b) before he has considered any representations made while that opportunity remains available which he is satisfied are either made by such employees or made on behalf of such employees by an organisation appearing to him to represent such employees.

(5) The reference in subsection (4)(a) above to employees of the Board affected by the withdrawal of service is a reference to persons who are employed by the Board for the purposes of, or in connection with, the service in question and who appear to the Secretary of State to be likely to be directly affected by the withdrawal of service.

(6) In any case other than one within subsection (1) or (3) above the Secretary of State shall revoke or vary the bus service condition in question in accordance with the Board's proposals if he is satisfied that adequate notice of those proposals was given in the notice published under section 120(1) of this Act in relation to the proposed withdrawal of service.

(7) Where in any case within subsection (1) or (3) above the Secretary of State revokes a bus service condition—

    (a) he may do so subject to such conditions as he thinks fit, including a condition requiring the Railways Board to secure the provision of an alternative service for the carriage of passengers by road ; and

    (b) he may from time to time give such directions to the Board as he thinks fit in connection with the withdrawal of the bus substitution service required by that condition ;

and, subject to section 119(4) of this Act, a condition imposed under paragraph (a) above may at any time be varied or revoked by the Secretary of State.

Supplementary and consequential provisions.

123.—(1) For the purposes of sections 120 to 122 of this Act and this section—

    (a) " Area Committee " means an Area Transport Users Consultative Committee established under section 56 of the 1962 Act or, in relation to the London area, the London Regional Passengers' Committee ;

(b) the appropriate Area Committee is the Area Committee for the area in which any locality or point affected by the proposed withdrawal of service is situated ; and

(c) " the Central Committee " means the Central Transport Consultative Committee for Great Britain established under section 56 of the 1962 Act.

In paragraph (a) above " the London area " means the area for which for the time being the London Regional Passengers' Committee act as an Area Transport Users Consultative Committee by virtue of section 41 of the London Regional Trans- 1984 c. 32. port Act 1984.

(2) Where objections with respect to any proposed withdrawal of service have been lodged with more than one Area Committee, the committees in question—

(a) may report to the Secretary of State jointly under section 121 of this Act ; or

(b) may agree that the consideration of objections and representations relating to the withdrawal and the making of a report to the Secretary of State shall be delegated to any of those committees appearing to them to be principally concerned ;

and references in sections 121 and 122 of this Act to a committee and to the appropriate Area Committee shall be read accordingly.

(3) Section 54(1) of the 1962 Act (advance information about railway and shipping closures) shall apply in relation to plans of the Railways Board for withdrawals of services (in the event of securing the necessary revocation or variation of the relevant bus service conditions) as it applies in relation to the Board's plans for closures.

(4) The duty of the Central Committee and of each Area Committee (other than the London Regional Passengers' Committee) under section 56(4) of the 1962 Act (duty to consider and make recommendations with respect to certain matters) shall apply to any matter affecting bus substitution services as it applies to any matter affecting the services and facilities provided by the Railways Board.

(5) References in sections 40 and 41 of the London Regional Transport Act 1984 (which deal with the functions of the London Regional Passengers' Committee) to services and facilities provided by the Railways Board or any subsidiary of theirs shall include references to bus substitution services.

(6) Nothing in section 56(4) of the 1962 Act or section 40(4) of the London Regional Transport Act 1984, as it has effect by virtue of subsection (4) or (5) above in relation to matters

affecting bus substitution services, shall entitle any committee to consider the charges made for any bus substitution service, or to consider any question relating to a withdrawal of service except as provided by section 121 of this Act.

(7) Section 56(13) of the 1962 Act (public hearings) shall apply in relation to hearings for the purposes of section 121(3) of this Act as it applies in relation to hearings for the purposes of subsection (9) of section 56 (objections to closures).

(8) In section 54(5) of the 1968 Act (power of Secretary of State to impose conditions in consenting to a closure)—

(a) at the beginning of paragraph (b) there shall be inserted the words " subject to section 119(4) of the Transport Act 1985 ";

(b) in paragraph (c), for the words from " as to the provision " to the end of the paragraph there shall be substituted the words " requiring the Railways Board to provide or (as the case may be) secure the provision of alternative services ; and " ;

(c) in paragraph (d), the words from " and to the Bus Company " to " Scottish Group " shall be omitted ; and

(d) in the words following paragraph (d), the words from " or, where " to " jointly " and the words from " or, as the case may be " to the end shall be omitted.

(9) Subsection (6) of that section shall be omitted, and in subsection (7), for the words " subsections (5) and (6) " there shall be substituted the words " subsection (5) ".

(10) In this section " closure " has the same meaning as in section 119 of this Act.

Reimbursement of Board's expenses in securing bus substitution services.
124.—(1) The Secretary of State may in respect of any period make grants to the Railways Board of such amounts as appear to him to be requisite for reimbursing the Board in respect of the net costs during that period of securing the provision of bus substitution services.

(2) The amount of those costs during any period shall be taken to be an amount equal to the difference between—

(a) the reduction in financial burden of the Board ; and

(b) the reduction in revenue of the Board ;

if the Board were not to secure the provision of those services during that period.

(3) Grants under this section require the approval of the
Treasury and may be made subject to such conditions as the
Secretary of State may, with the approval of the Treasury,
think fit.

The Disabled Persons Transport Advisory Committee

125.—(1) There shall be established in accordance with this   The Disabled
section a body to be known as the Disabled Persons Transport   Persons
Advisory Committee.   Transport
   Advisory
(2) The Committee shall consist of—   Committee
   and Secretary
    (*a*) a chairman appointed by the Secretary of State ; and   of State's

    (*b*) not less than ten, nor more than twenty, other members   Guidance.
        appointed by the Secretary of State after consultation
        with such bodies as appear to him to be representative
        of the interests of persons likely to be significantly
        concerned with matters within the competence of the
        Committee.

(3) The Secretary of State shall, so far as is reasonably
practicable, secure that at all times at least half of the membership of the Committee consists of persons who are disabled.

(4) The Secretary of State may appoint one or more members
of the Committee to be deputy chairman or (as the case may be)
deputy chairmen of the Committee.

(5) It shall be the duty of the Committee to consider any
matter, relating to the needs of disabled persons in connection
with public passenger transport, which is referred to them by the
Secretary of State or which they think it appropriate to consider
without such a reference and to give such advice to the Secretary
of State on any matter which they have considered as they think
appropriate.

(6) The Committee shall make an annual report to the Secretary of State, who shall lay a copy of it before each House of
Parliament.

(7) The Secretary of State shall from time to time issue
guidance as to measures that may be taken with a view to—

    (*a*) making access to vehicles used in the provision of public
        passenger transport services by road easier for disabled
        persons; and

    (*b*) making such vehicles better adapted to the needs of
        disabled persons.

(8) The Secretary of State shall consult the Committee before
issuing any such guidance.

(9) Schedule 5 to this Act shall have effect with respect to
the Committee.

Application of
sections 52 and
56 of the 1981
Act.

Provisions supplementary to Parts I and II

126·—(1) The power under section 52(1) of the 1981 Act (fees for grant of licences, etc.) to prescribe fees chargeable by traffic commissioners shall apply in relation to fees so chargeable in respect of—

(a) applications for the registration of services under section 6 of this Act and for the variation of such registrations ;

(b) the issue of any documents issued in accordance with regulations under that section with respect to registrations under that section ;

(c) applications for, and the grant of, permits under section 19 or 22 of this Act ; and

(d) applications for, and the grant of, London local service licences.

(2) Subsection (2) of that section (power of traffic commissioners to decline to proceed until any fee or instalment of a fee is paid) shall accordingly apply as if subsection (1) above were included in subsection (1) of that section ; and for that purpose the references in subsection (2) of that section to licences shall include references to permits.

(3) Section 56 of the 1981 Act (records of licences) shall apply in relation to—

(a) registrations under section 6 of this Act ;

(b) traffic regulation conditions determined under section 7 of this Act ; and

(c) London local service licences granted under Part II of this Act ;

as it applies in relation to licences granted under that Act.

Offences and
legal
proceedings.

127.—(1) Section 65 of the 1981 Act (forgery and misuse of documents) shall apply to the following documents, namely—

(a) a permit under section 19 or 22 of this Act ; and

(b) a London local service licence.

(2) Section 66 of that Act (false statements to obtain licence, etc.) shall apply in relation to a false statement for the purpose of obtaining the grant of any such permit or licence as it applies in relation to a false statement for the purposes there mentioned.

(3) Section 67 of that Act (penalty for breach of regulations under that Act) shall have effect as if Parts I and II of this Act were contained in that Act.

(4) The defence provided by section 68(3) of that Act (that the person charged took all reasonable precautions and exercised all due diligence to avoid the commission of an offence under

certain provisions of that Act) shall apply in relation to an offence under any of the following provisions of this Act, that is to say, sections 23(5), 30(2), 35(6) and 38(7).

(5) The provisions of that Act mentioned in subsection (6) below shall apply in relation to an offence, or (as the case may be) in relation to proceedings for an offence, under Part I or II of this Act as they apply in relation to an offence, or in relation to proceedings for an offence, under Part II of that Act.

(6) Those provisions are—

> section 69 (restriction on institution in England or Wales of proceedings for an offence under Part II) ;

> section 70 (duty to give information as to identity of driver in certain cases) ;

> section 71 (evidence by certificate in proceedings in England or Wales for an offence under Part II) ;

> section 72 (proof in summary proceedings in England or Wales of identity of driver of vehicle) ; and

> section 74 (offences under Part II committed by companies).

(7) Section 75 of that Act (destination of fines in respect of certain offences committed in Scotland) shall have effect as if Part I of this Act were contained in provisions of that Act preceding section 75.

128.—(1) The provisions of the 1981 Act mentioned in subsection (2) below shall have effect as if Parts I and II of this Act were contained in that Act. *Further supplementary provisions.*

(2) Those provisions are—

> sections 76 and 77 (power of Secretary of State to hold inquiries for the purposes of that Act and general provisions as to inquiries so held) ; and

> section 85 (nothing in that Act to authorise a nuisance).

General supplementary provisions

129.—(1) This section applies to any scheme under section 50(2), 59, 61(9) or 68 of this Act (referred to below in this section as a transfer scheme). *Transfer schemes.*

(2) A transfer scheme may define the property, rights and liabilities to be transferred by the scheme—

> (a) by specifying the property, rights or liabilities in question ; or

> (b) by referring to all the property, rights and liabilities comprised in the whole or any specified part of the transferor's undertaking ;

(or partly in one way and partly in the other) and may contain such supplementary, incidental and consequential provisions as may appear to the authority making the scheme to be necessary or expedient (including in particular, but without prejudice to the generality of that, provision with respect to the consideration to be provided by the transferee for any transfer under the scheme).

(3) Subject to the following provisions of this section, Schedule 4 to the 1968 Act (supplementary provisions as to certain transfers of property, rights and liabilities) shall apply to any transfer under section 50(4), 59(7), 61(11) or 68(7) of this Act ; and each of those provisions shall have effect subject to the provisions of that Schedule.

(4) In Schedule 4 as it applies by virtue of subsection (3) above—

(a) any reference to a transfer by or a vesting by virtue of that Act shall be read as a reference to a transfer by or a vesting by virtue of the transfer scheme in question ; and

(b) the reference in paragraph 13(5) to the relevant provisions of that Act shall be read as including a reference to the relevant provisions of this Act.

(5) The Secretary of State may by order make modifications in Schedule 4 for the purposes of its application to transfers under section 50(4), 59(7), 61(11) or 68(7) of this Act.

Corporation tax and capital gains tax.
1970 c. 24.

130.—(1) Section 16(1)(a) of the Finance Act 1970 (which excludes precept income and grants in computing the profits of a Passenger Transport Executive chargeable to corporation tax) shall not apply with respect to any accounting period beginning on or after the passing of this Act.

(2) In computing for the purposes of the Corporation Tax Acts the profit or loss of a Passenger Transport Executive for any accounting period beginning on or after the passing of this Act, the loss of any earlier accounting period shall be computed as if section 16(1)(a) of the Finance Act 1970 had not been enacted.

1979 c. 14.

(3) For the purposes of the Capital Gains Tax Act 1979, the transfer under section 59(8) or section 85(4) of this Act of any asset from a Passenger Transport Executive to a Passenger Transport Authority shall be deemed to be for a consideration such that no gain or loss accrues to the Executive ; and Schedule 5 to that Act (assets held on 6th April 1965) shall have effect in relation to any asset so transferred as if the acquisition or provision of it by the Executive had been the acquisition or provision of it by the Authority.

(4) If, under section 59 of this Act, a company is formed by a Passenger Transport Executive and the shares in or securities

of that company are subsequently transferred to a Passenger Transport Authority, section 278 of the Income and Corporation Taxes Act 1970 (deemed disposals of assets for capital gains purposes where member leaves group) shall not have effect as respects any of the assets of the company on its ceasing to be a 75 per cent. subsidiary (within the meaning of the Tax Acts) of the Executive. PART VI
1970 c. 10.

131.—(1) Stamp duty shall not be chargeable under section 47 of the Finance Act 1973 in respect of— Stamp duty.
1973 c. 51.

> (a) the formation of a subsidiary of the National Bus Company ; or
>
> (b) any increase in the capital of such a subsidiary ;

if the transaction concerned is certified by the Treasury as satisfying the requirements of subsections (3) and (4) below.

(2) Stamp duty shall not be so chargeable in respect of the formation of any company in pursuance of section 59(1), 61(8) or 67(1) of this Act, if the formation of the company is certified by the Treasury—

> (a) as being effected in pursuance of any of those provisions ; and
>
> (b) as satisfying the requirements of subsection (4) below.

(3) A transaction satisfies the requirements of this subsection if it is effected solely for the purpose of facilitating the eventual implementation of any disposal required in pursuance of the National Bus Company's disposal programme under Part III of this Act.

(4) A transaction satisfies the requirements of this subsection if it is entered into solely in connection with a relevant transfer, takes place on or before the transfer date and does not give rise to an excess of capital.

In this subsection, " relevant transfer " means—

> (a) in a case within subsection (1) above, a transfer to be effected under section 50 of this Act ;
>
> (b) in a case within subsection (2) above, a transfer to be effected in pursuance of a scheme made under section 59, 61(9) or 68 of this Act.

(5) For the purposes of subsection (4) above a transaction gives rise to an excess of capital if—

> (a) in a case falling within subsection (1)(a) or (2) above the total issued capital of the subsidiary or (as the case may be) of the company in question exceeds, on the transfer date, the total value of the assets less liabilities transferred ; or

(*b*) in a case falling within subsection (1)(*b*) above the aggregate amount of the increase of issued capital of the subsidiary exceeds, on that date, that total value ; and in this subsection " issued capital " means issued share capital or loan capital.

(6) Stamp duty shall not be chargeable—

(*a*) on any scheme made under section 50(2) of this Act or on any scheme or order made under any provision of Part IV of this Act ; or

(*b*) on any instrument which is certified to the Commissioners of Inland Revenue by the transferring authority or (as the case may be) by both or all the transferring authorities as having been made or executed in pursuance of Schedule 4 to the 1968 Act as it applies by virtue of any provision of this Act in relation to a transfer in pursuance of any such scheme or order ; or

(*c*) on any instrument which is so certified as having been made or executed for the purpose of giving effect to any transfer authorised by section 50(1) or (as the case may be) required under section 59(8) of this Act.

(7) No such instrument as is mentioned in subsection (6)(*b*) or (*c*) above shall be treated as duly stamped unless it is stamped with the duty to which it would but for subsection (6) above be liable or it has, in accordance with the provisions of section 12 of the Stamp Act 1891, been stamped with a particular stamp denoting that it is not chargeable with any duty or that it is duly stamped.

1891 c. 39.

Operation of vehicles, etc., by partnerships.

132. Section 58(1) of the 1981 Act (power to modify the provisions of that Act in their application to the operation of vehicles and the provision of services by persons in partnership) shall apply in relation to the provisions of this Act.

Functions of Passenger Transport Authorities and Executives: supplementary.

133.—(1) In Part II of the 1968 Act, the references to that Part of that Act or (as the case may be) to that Act mentioned in subsection (2) below shall include references to this Act.

(2) Those references are—

(*a*) the references to that Part of that Act in section 12(2), (3)(*d*) and (*g*) (borrowing powers of Executive) and in section 15(5) (expenditure by Authority in performing their functions to be defrayed by Executive) ; and

(*b*) the reference to that Act in section 12(5)(*b*) (which refers to rights of priority in respect of any liability assumed by or transferred to an Executive in pursuance of that Act).

Regulations, rules and orders.

134.—(1) Section 60 of the 1981 Act (general power to make regulations for purposes of that Act) shall have effect as if Parts I and II of this Act were contained in that Act.

(2) In that section—

(a) in subsection (1) (which, in effect, provides that all regulations authorised under that Act are to be made under that section) the words from " for any purpose " to " generally " and the words from " and regulations under this section " to the end of the subsection shall be omitted ;

(b) the following subsection shall be inserted after subsection (1)—

" (1A) Regulations made under any provision of this Act may make different provision for different cases to which the regulations apply, and may in particular—

(a) make different provision as respects different areas ; and

(b) make different provision as respects different classes or descriptions of vehicles or as respects the same class or description of vehicles in different circumstances." ;

(c) in subsection (2) (which defines " regulations " as meaning regulations under that section), for the words " under this section " there shall be substituted the words " by the Secretary of State " ; and

(d) subsection (3) (which excepts certain provisions of that Act from being included in references to that Act in that section and is unnecessary in view of the amendments made above in this section) shall be omitted.

(3) The power to make regulations under that section, as it applies by virtue of this section, shall extend to any of the following matters—

(a) applications for, and the issue of, permits under section 19 or 22 of this Act ; and

(b) the issue of copies of such permits in the case of permits lost or destroyed.

(4) The Secretary of State may make regulations under this section for the purpose of carrying the provisions of this Act (apart from Parts I and II) into effect.

(5) Regulations or rules made under any provision of this Act (other than one contained in Part I or II), and any order made by the Secretary of State under any provision of this Act (including one so contained), may make different provision for different cases to which those regulations or rules or (as the case may be) to which that order applies, and may in particular make different provision as respects different areas.

G

PART VI
Procedure for
making
regulations,
rules and
orders.

135.—(1) Section 61 of the 1981 Act (procedure for making regulations under that Act) shall have effect as if Parts I and II of this Act were contained in that Act; and in subsection (2) of that section (duty to consult before making regulations under section 59 or 60 of that Act) the words "section 59 or 60 of" shall be omitted.

(2) Any power of the Secretary of State—

    (*a*) to make regulations or rules under any provision of this Act (other than one contained in Part I or II); or

    (*b*) to make an order under any provision of this Act (including one so contained);

shall be exercisable by statutory instrument.

(3) Subject to subsection (4) below, any statutory instrument containing any such regulations, rules or order shall be subject to annulment in pursuance of a resolution of either House of Parliament.

(4) Subsection (3) above does not apply to a statutory instrument containing an order under section 46, 52(5), 53(1), 85 or 140(2) of this Act.

Directions.

136.—(1) It shall be the duty of any person to whom the Secretary of State gives directions under this Act to give effect to those directions.

(2) Any direction given by the Secretary of State under any provision of this Act (including a direction specifying a period or date for any purposes of Part IV of this Act) may be varied or revoked by a subsequent direction given under that provision.

(3) Any direction given by the Secretary of State under this Act shall be in writing.

General
interpretation.
1962 c. 46.
1972 c. 70.
1968 c. 73.
1981 c. 14.

137.—(1) In this Act, unless the context otherwise requires—

" the 1962 Act " means the Transport Act 1962;

" the 1972 Act " means the Local Government Act 1972;

" the 1968 Act " means the Transport Act 1968;

" the 1981 Act " means the Public Passenger Vehicles Act 1981;

" body " means a body of persons, whether corporate or unincorporate;

" bus service condition " has the meaning given by section 119(4) of this Act;

" bus substitution service " has the meaning given by section 119(1) of this Act;

" employees' share scheme " means a scheme for encouraging or facilitating the holding of shares or debentures in a company by or for the benefit of—

(a) the bona fide employees or former employees of the company or of a subsidiary of the company ; or

(b) the wives, husbands, widows, widowers or children or step-children under the age of eighteen of such employees or former employees ;

" equity share capital " has the meaning given in the Companies Act 1985 ;

" excursion or tour " means a service for the carriage of passengers by road at separate fares on which the passengers travel together on a journey, with or without breaks, from one or more places to one or more other places and back ;

" functions " includes powers, duties and obligations ;

" interest " means, in relation to a company's share capital of any description, a beneficial interest (whether held directly or through nominees or subsidiaries) in that share capital ;

" liability " includes an obligation ;

" local service " has the meaning given by section 2 of this Act ;

" London " means the administrative area of Greater London as for the time being constituted ;

" London local service " has the meaning given by section 34(1) of this Act ;

" pension ", in relation to a person, means a pension, whether contributory or not, of any kind whatsoever payable to or in respect of him, and includes—

(a) a gratuity so payable ;

(b) a return of contributions to a pension fund, with or without interest on or any other addition to those contributions ; and

(c) any sums payable on or in respect of the death of that person ;

" pension rights " includes, in relation to any person, all forms of right to or eligibility for the present or future payment of a pension, and any expectation of the accruer of a pension under any customary practice, and includes a right of allocation in respect of the present or future payment of a pension ;

" prescribed " means prescribed by regulations ;

G 2

" public passenger transport services " has the meaning given by section 63(10)(*a*) of this Act ;

" the Railways Board " means the British Railways Board established under section 1 of the 1962 Act ;

" regulations " means regulations made by the Secretary of State ;

" securities ", in relation to a body corporate, means any shares, stock, debentures, debenture stock, and any other security of a similar nature, of the body corporate ;

" social services functions " means functions which are social services functions for the purposes of the Local Authority Social Services Act 1970 ;

" social work functions " means functions which are social work functions for the purposes of the Social Work (Scotland) Act 1968 ;

" the standard scale " has the meaning given by section 75 of the Criminal Justice Act 1982 ;

" stopping place " means, in relation to any service or part of a service, a point at which passengers are (or, in the case of a proposed service, are proposed to be) taken up or set down in the course of that service or part ;

" subsidiary " means, in relation to any body corporate, a body corporate which is a subsidiary of the first-mentioned body corporate as defined by section 736 of the Companies Act 1985 (taking references in that section to a company as being references to a body corporate) ;

" traffic area " means a traffic area constituted for the purposes of the 1981 Act, and section 80 of that Act shall apply to references in this Act to the Metropolitan Traffic Area ;

" trunk road " has the meaning given by section 329 of the Highways Act 1980 or, as respects Scotland, section 151 of the Roads (Scotland) Act 1984 ;

" wholly-owned subsidiary " means a subsidiary all the securities of which are owned by a body corporate of which it is a subsidiary, or by one or more other wholly-owned subsidiaries of that body, or partly by that body and partly by any wholly-owned subsidiary of that body ;

and the expressions listed in subsection (2) below have the same meaning as in the 1981 Act.

(2) Those expressions are—

" company " ;

1970 c. 42.
1968 c. 49.
1982 c. 48.
1985 c. 6.
1980 c. 66.
1984 c. 54.

" contravention " ;

" fares " ;

" modification " ;

" operator " (in references to the operator of a vehicle) ;

" operating centre " ;

" PSV operator's licence " ;

" public service vehicle " ;

" road " ;

" statutory provision " ; and

" traffic commissioner ".

(3) References in this Act to a vehicle's being used for carrying passengers for hire or reward shall be read in accordance with section 1(5) of the 1981 Act.

(4) References in this Act to agreements providing for service subsidies shall be read in accordance with section 63(10)(*b*) of this Act.

(5) References in this Act to Passenger Transport Authorities and Executives and to passenger transport areas are references respectively to the Passenger Transport Authorities and Executives, and to passenger transport areas, for the purposes of Part II of the 1968 Act.

(6) References in this Act, in relation to a bus substitution service, to the withdrawal of service shall be read in accordance with section 120(1) of this Act (and references to a withdrawal of service or to withdrawals of service have a corresponding meaning).

(7) For the purposes of this Act the operator of a passenger transport service of any description is the person, or each of the persons, providing the service ; and for those purposes the operator of a vehicle being used on a road for the carriage of passengers for hire or reward at separate fares shall be taken to be providing the service provided by means of the vehicle unless he proves that the service is or forms part of a service provided not by himself but by one or more other persons.

(8) For the purposes of this Act an interest in a company's equity share capital is a controlling interest if it subsists in more than half in nominal value of that capital.

138. The following are authorised by this section—   Expenses and

    (*a*) the payment out of money provided by Parliament of receipts.
        any expenditure incurred by the Secretary of State
        under section 54(4) of or paragraph 7 of Schedule 4
        to this Act or in making grants under section 108, 109
        or 124 of this Act ;

(b) any increase in payments out of money so provided arising from any increase in administrative expenses of the Secretary of State or the expenses of local authorities attributable to the provisions of this Act ; and

(c) any increase attributable to this Act in the sums payable into the Consolidated Fund by virtue of section 52(3) or 75 of the 1981 Act (fees received by traffic commissioners and certain fines to be paid into the Consolidated Fund).

Transitional provisions, savings, amendments, repeals and revocation.

139.—(1) This Act shall have effect subject to the transitional provisions and savings set out in Schedule 6 to this Act.

(2) The enactments mentioned in Schedule 7 to this Act shall have effect subject to the amendments specified in that Schedule (which are minor amendments and amendments consequential on the provisions of this Act).

(3) The enactments mentioned in Schedule 8 to this Act (which include certain provisions which are already spent) are repealed to the extent specified in the third column of that Schedule.

(4) Without prejudice to section 13 of this Act, the Secretary of State may, for the purpose of taking account of any of the provisions of Part I of this Act, by order modify or repeal any provision made by any local Act passed before the commencement of this subsection.

S.I. 1976/98.

(5) Paragraph 4(2) of the Schedule to the Restrictive Trade Practices (Services) Order 1976 is revoked.

Short title, commencement and extent.

140.—(1) This Act may be cited as the Transport Act 1985.

(2) This Act (apart from this section, section 58 of this Act and paragraph 12 of Schedule 6 to this Act) shall come into force on such day or days as the Secretary of State may by order appoint, and different days may be appointed for different purposes (including different purposes of the same provision).

(3) An order under subsection (2) above may contain such transitional provisions and savings (whether or not involving the modification of any statutory provision) as appear to the Secretary of State necessary or expedient in connection with the provisions brought (wholly or partly) into force by the order.

(4) The following provisions of this Act do not extend to Scotland, that is to say—

sections 10 and 11 ;

Part II ; and

section 102.

(5) This Act, with the exceptions mentioned in subsection (6) below, does not extend to Northern Ireland.

(6) Those exceptions are—

section 114(1)(*a*) and (2) ; and

section 115.

SCHEDULES

SCHEDULE 1

AMENDMENTS CONSEQUENTIAL ON THE ABOLITION OF ROAD SERVICE LICENSING

The Transport Act 1968

1. In section 159(1) of the Transport Act 1968 (interpretation)—

(a) for the definition of " bus service " there shall be substituted the following—

" ' bus service ' means a local service other than one on which the passengers travel together on a journey, with or without breaks, from one or more places to one or more places and back " ; and

(b) the following definition shall be inserted at the appropriate place—

" ' local service ' has the same meaning as in the Transport Act 1985 ; ".

The Local Government (*Miscellaneous Provisions*) Act 1976

2. In section 63(3)(b) of the Local Government (Miscellaneous Provisions) Act 1976 for the words " road service licence " there shall be substituted the words " local service within the meaning of the Transport Act 1985 ".

The Energy Act 1976

3.—(1) Paragraph 1 of Schedule 1 to the Energy Act 1976 (relaxation of road traffic and transport law) shall be amended as follows.

(2) In sub-paragraph (1), for the words from " any ", where it first occurs, to " contract carriage " there shall be substituted the words " a local service within the meaning of the Transport Act 1985 or use any public service vehicle on a road for carrying passengers for hire or reward ".

(3) In sub-paragraph (1), after paragraph (a) there shall be inserted the following paragraph—

" (aa) without complying with the requirements of sections 6 (registration of local services outside London) and 35 (provision of local services within London under London local service licences) of the 1985 Act ; "

(4) In sub-paragraph (1)(c) the words " or Part III " shall be omitted and after " 1981 " there shall be inserted the words " or Part I or II of the Transport Act 1985 ".

(5) In sub-paragraph (2), the words " section 60 of ", and the words from " general " to first " vehicles ", shall be omitted and after " 1981 " there shall be inserted " or Part I of the Transport Act 1985 ".

The Public Passenger Vehicles Act 1981

4. In section 12 of the 1981 Act (PSV operator's licence), for subsection (1) there shal be substituted the following subsection—

" (1) A public service vehicle shall not be used on a road for carrying passengers for hire or reward except under a PSV operator's licence granted in accordance with the following provisions of this Part of this Act.".

5. In section 22(1) of that Act (prohibition on driving a public service vehicle on a road without a licence to drive a public service vehicle or employing unlicensed persons for the purpose), for the words " a stage, express or contract carriage " there shall be substituted the words " a public service vehicle being used on a road for carrying passengers for hire or reward.".

6. In section 46 of that Act (fare-paying passengers on school buses)—

　　(*a*) in subsection (1)(*b*), the word " bus ", where it occurs in the expression " local bus service ", shall be omitted ; and

　　(*b*) in subsection (3), the definition of " local bus service " shall be omitted.

7. In section 52(1)(*a*)(i) of that Act (fees for grant of PSV operators' licences and road service licences etc.) the words " and road service licences " shall be omitted.

8. In section 53(1) of that Act (payment of expenses), for the words " II or III " there shall be substituted the words " or II ".

9. In sections 57 and 58 of that Act (death, etc. of licence holder, and provision with respect to partnerships and related matters), the words " or road service licence " (in each place where they occur) shall be omitted.

10. In section 59 of that Act (power to make regulations as to procedure on applications for licences)—

　　(*a*) in paragraph (*a*) the words " road service licences " ; and

　　(*b*) in paragraph (*b*) the words " or road service licences " ; shall be omitted.

11. In section 68(4)(*a*) of that Act (provisions to which a defence under subsection (3) of that section applies), for the words " 27(2) and 30(6) and (7) " there shall be substituted the words " and 27(2) ".

12. Section 81(2) of that Act (definition for purposes of that Act of the operator of a stage or express carriage service) shall cease to have effect.

13. In section 82(1) of that Act (definitions of expressions used in that Act) the definitions of the following expressions shall be omitted—

　　" contract carriage " ;

　　" excursion or tour " ;

　　" express carriage " and " express carriage service " ;

　　" road service licence " ;

　　" stage carriage " and " stage carriage service " ; and

　　" trial area " ;

SCH. 1   and after the definition of "local authority" there shall be inserted
the following definition—

> " " local service " has the same meaning as in the Transport
> Act 1985 ; ".

14. In section 83 of that Act (construction of references in other
Acts to public service vehicles, etc.)—

> (*a*) in subsection (1), the words " " stage carriage ", " express
> carriage " or " contract carriage " " ; and
>
> (*b*) subsection (2) ;

shall be omitted.

1984 c. 27.   *The Road Traffic Regulation Act 1984*

15.—(1) The Road Traffic Regulation Act 1984 shall be amended
as follows.

(2) In section 7(5) (restriction on the right to appeal from road
service licensing decisions of traffic commissioners in any case where
the decision is certified to be necessary to secure conformity with
a traffic regulation order), for the words from "traffic commissioners " to " the commissioners " there shall be substituted the
words " traffic commissioner for the Metropolitan Traffic Area under
section 42 of the Transport Act 1985 in the case of a decision of
his with respect to a London local service licence if and so far as he
certifies ".

(3) In section 10—

> (*a*) in subsection (4) (restriction on the right to appeal from
> road service licensing decisions of traffic commissioners
> in any case where the decision is certified to be necessary
> to secure conformity with an experimental traffic order),
> for the words from " traffic commissioners " to " the com-
> missioners " there shall be substituted the words " com-
> missioner for the Metropolitan Traffic Area under section
> 42 of the Transport Act 1985 in the case of a decision of
> the commissioner with respect to a London local service
> licence if and so far as he certifies " ; and
>
> (*b*) after subsection (5) there shall be inserted the following
> subsection—
>
>> " (6) The reference in subsection (4) above to the
>> Metropolitan Traffic Area shall be construed as if it
>> were contained in the Public Passenger Vehicles Act
>> 1981."

(4) In section 142(1) (interpretation), in the definition of " public
service vehicle ", for the words " and ' stage carriage ' have the
same meanings " there shall be substituted the words " has the same
meaning ".

(5) In Schedule 9—

> (*a*) in paragraph 13(3)(*b*), for the words " stage carriage "
> there shall be substituted the words " vehicle being used in
> the provision of a local service within the meaning of the
> Transport Act 1985 " ; and

(*b*) in paragraph 13(3)(*c*)(i), there shall be substituted for the words from " stage carriage ", where they first occur, to " 1981 " the words " local service (within the meaning of the Transport Act 1985) " and for the words " stage carriage ", where they next occur, the word " vehicle ".

16.—(1) Subject to any provision made by or under this Act, in any enactment or instrument passed or made before the commencement of section 1 of this Act—

(*a*) any reference to a stage carriage service shall be construed as a reference to a local service ;

(*b*) any reference to an express carriage service shall be construed as a reference to any service for the carriage of passengers for hire or reward at separate fares which is neither a local service nor one provided by a vehicle to which sub-paragraph (2) below applies ;

(*c*) any reference to a stage carriage shall be construed as a reference to a public service vehicle being used in the provision of a local service ;

(*d*) any reference to an express carriage shall be construed as a reference to a public service vehicle being used to carry passengers for hire or reward at separate fares other than one being used in the provision of a local service ; and

(*e*) any reference to a contract carriage shall be construed as a reference to a public service vehicle being used to carry passengers for hire or reward otherwise than at separate fares.

(2) When used in circumstances in which the conditions set out in Part III of Schedule 1 to the 1981 Act are fulfilled, a public service vehicle carrying passengers at separate fares shall be treated, for the purposes of any enactment or instrument to which paragraph (*d*) or (*e*) of sub-paragraph (1) above applies, as being used to carry passengers otherwise than at separate fares.

SCHEDULE 2

AMENDMENTS CONSEQUENTIAL ON SECTION 3

PART I

SCHEDULE SUBSTITUTED FOR SCHEDULE 2 TO THE 1981 ACT

" **SCHEDULE 2**

TRAFFIC COMMISSIONERS

Terms of service of traffic commissioners

1. The Secretary of State may remove a traffic commissioner from his office for inability or misbehaviour.

2. If a traffic commissioner acquires a financial interest in a transport undertaking which carries passengers or goods by road within Great Britain he shall, within four weeks after so doing, give notice of that acquisition in writing to the Secretary of State specifying the interest so acquired and the Secretary of State, after taking the matter into consideration, may if he thinks fit declare that the traffic commissioner has vacated his office.

Appointment and terms of office of deputies to traffic commissioners

3. In the case of illness, incapacity or absence of a traffic commissioner, the Secretary of State may appoint some other person to act as his deputy.

4. If the Secretary of State considers that the duties to be performed by a traffic commissioner, or any deputy appointed under paragraph 3 above to the traffic commissioner, cannot conveniently or efficiently be performed by one person, the Secretary of State may appoint one or more persons to act as deputy to the traffic commissioner.

5. A person appointed under paragraph 4 above shall be appointed upon such terms and conditions, including conditions as to the time which he is to devote to the duties of his office, as the Secretary of State may determine, and shall act for the traffic commissioner whose deputy he is in such matters as the traffic commissioner, or any deputy appointed by reason of the traffic commissioner's illness, incapacity or absence, may from time to time direct or as the Secretary of State may from time to time by general directions require, and for that purpose shall exercise and perform all the powers and duties of the traffic commissioner.

6.—(1) Where the office of traffic commissioner for any traffic area becomes vacant the Secretary of State may, pending the appointment of a new traffic commissioner for that area under section 4 of this Act, appoint a person (whether or not over the age of sixty-five) under this paragraph to act as traffic commissioner for that area for a limited period.

(2) Any person appointed under sub-paragraph (1) above shall—

(*a*) hold office for such period as the Secretary of State specifies when making the appointment ; and

(*b*) during that period be treated for all purposes (except those of paragraph 9 below) as the traffic commissioner for the traffic area in question.

Staff of traffic commissioners

7. Subject to the approval of the Treasury, the Secretary of State may appoint such persons to act as officers and servants of a traffic commissioner as he considers appropriate.

Remuneration and pensions

8. There shall be paid to a traffic commissioner and deputy traffic commissioner, and to the persons acting as officers or servants of a traffic commissioner, such remuneration and allowances as may be determined by the Secretary of State with the consent of the Treasury.

9. The principal civil service pension scheme (within the meaning of section 2 of the Superannuation Act 1972) which is for the time being in force shall apply to persons holding the office of traffic commissioner for each of the traffic areas."

Part II
Further Consequential Amendments
The Transport Act 1968

1972 c. 11.

1968 c. 73.

1.—(1) The Transport Act 1968 shall be amended as follows.

(2) In section 96(10)(*b*), there shall be substituted for the words "commissioners or licensing authority" the word "commissioner" and for the words "commissioners or authority think" the words "commissioner thinks".

(3) In section 98(3), there shall be substituted for the words "commissioners or licensing authority" in both places the word "commissioner" and for the words "commissioners or authority think" the words "commissioner thinks".

(4) In section 99, there shall be substituted for the words "commissioners or licensing authority" in subsections (1) and (8) the word "commissioner".

(5) In section 103(5), for the words "commissioners or licensing authority" there shall be substituted the word "commissioner".

The Tribunals and Inquiries Act 1971

1971 c. 62.

2.—(1) The Tribunals and Inquiries Act 1971 shall be amended as follows.

(2) In Part I of Schedule 1 (tribunals under direct supervision of the Council on Tribunals), for paragraph 30 there shall be substituted the following paragraph—

"Road Traffic.   30. The traffic commissioner for any area constituted for the purposes of the Public Passenger Vehicles Act 1981 (c. 14)."

(3) In Part II of Schedule 1 (equivalent provision for Scotland), in paragraph 48, there shall be substituted for the word "commissioners" the word "commissioner" and for the word "their" the word "his".

The Road Traffic Act 1972

1972 c. 20.

3.—(1) In section 113(1) of the Road Traffic Act 1972 (licensing authority for Part IV of that Act), there shall be substituted—

(*a*) for the words "The person who is the chairman of the traffic commissioners" the words "The traffic commissioner"; and

(*b*) for the words from "including" to "duty" the words "shall exercise the function".

(2) In section 123 of that Act there shall be substituted for the words "the traffic commissioners" the words "a traffic commissioner".

(3) In section 124 of that Act, for the words "traffic commissioners" there shall be substituted the words "traffic commissioner".

The Public Passenger Vehicles Act 1981

4.—(1) The Public Passenger Vehicles Act 1981 shall be amended as follows.

(2) In section 3(3), for the word "commissioners", whenever occurring, there shall be substituted the word "commissioner".

(3) In section 9(8), for the word "commissioners" there shall be substituted in both places the word "commissioner".

(4) In section 12, there shall be substituted—

(a) for the word "commissioners", whenever occurring, the word "commissioner";

(b) in subsection (3), for the words "different areas" the words "a different area"; and

(c) in subsection (4), for the word "they" the word "he".

(5) In section 14 (grant of licences)—

(a) for the word "commissioners", whenever occurring, there shall be substituted the word "commissioner";

(b) in subsections (1) and (3), for the word "are" in each place (other than where it first occurs in subsection (3)) there shall be substituted the word "is";

(c) in subsection (4), there shall be substituted for the word "determine" the word "determines" and for the word "they" the word "he".

(6) In section 15, there shall be substituted—

(a) in subsection (1), for the word "commissioners" the word "commissioner" and for the word "consider" the word "considers";

(b) in subsection (2), for the words "Traffic commissioners" the words "A traffic commissioner", for the word "commissioners", in the second place where it occurs, the word "commissioner" and for the words "the commissioners", where they last occur, the word "him";

(c) in subsection (3), for the word "commissioners" the word "commissioner"; and

(d) in subsection (4), for the word "commissioners", where it first occurs, the word "commissioner", for the words "commissioners decide" the words "commissioner decides" and for the words "they" and "them" the words "he" and "him".

(7) In section 16, there shall be substituted—

> (*a*) in subsection (1), for the words "Traffic commissioners" the words "A traffic commissioner" and for the words "those commissioners" the words "that commissioner";
>
> (*b*) in subsection (3), for the words "Traffic commissioners" the words "A traffic commissioner" and for the word "them" the word "him" and for the words "they think" the words "he thinks";
>
> (*c*) in subsection (5), for the word "commissioners" the word "commissioner" and for the words "they think" the words "he thinks";
>
> (*d*) in subsection (6) for the word "commissioners" in both places the word "commissioner", for the word "their" in both places the word "his" and for the word "they" the word "he";
>
> (*e*) in subsection (8), for the word "commissioners" the word "commissioner" and for the words "they are" the words "he is"; and
>
> (*f*) in subsection (9), for the word "commissioners" in both places the word "commissioner".

(8) In section 17, there shall be substituted—

> (*a*) in subsection (1), for the word "commissioners" the word "commissioner" and for the word "them" the word "him";
>
> (*b*) in subsection (2), for the word "commissioners" where it first occurs the word "commissioner" and for the words "the commissioners direct" the words "he directs";
>
> (*c*) in subsection (4), for the words "Traffic commissioners" the words "A traffic commissioner" and for the word "them" the word "him"; and
>
> (*d*) in subsection (5), for the words "traffic commissioners decide" the words "a traffic commissioner decides" and for the words "they" and "them" the words "he" and "him".

(9) In section 18(2) there shall be substituted for the words "Traffic commissioners" the words "A traffic commissioner" and for the word "commissioners" the word "commissioner".

(10) In section 19, there shall be substituted—

> (*a*) in subsections (1), (2) and (3), for the word "commissioners" the word "commissioner"; and
>
> (*b*) in subsection (4) for the words "Traffic commissioners" the words "A traffic commissioner", for the word "them" in each place the word "him" and for the word "his" the words "the holder's".

(11) In section 20, there shall be substituted—

> (*a*) in subsection (3), for the word "commissioners" where first occurring the word "commissioner", for the words "those commissioners" in both places the words "that

commissioner ", for the word " them " in each place the word " him ", for the word " they " in both places the word " he ", for the word " him ", in both places in paragraph (*a*), the words " the holder " and for the word " him ", in paragraph (*b*), the words " the holder or former holder " ; and

(*b*) in subsection (6), for the word " commissioners " the word " commissioner ".

(12) In section 21, there shall be substituted—

(*a*) for the word " commissioners ", whenever occurring, the word " commissioner " ;

(*b*) in subsection (2), for the words " they " and " their " the words " he " and " his " ; and

(*c*) in subsection (3), for the words " they are satisfied they " the words " he is satisfied he " and for the word " them " the words " the commissioner ".

(13) In section 23—

(*a*) in subsection (1), there shall be substituted for the words " the traffic commissioners " the words " a traffic commissioner ", and for the word " commissioners " the word " commissioner " and for the word " them " the word " him " ;

(*b*) in subsection (2), for the word " commissioners " in both places there shall be substituted the word " commissioner ".

(14) In section 52, there shall be substituted—

(*a*) in subsection (1), for the word " commissioners " whenever occurring the word " commissioner " ;

(*b*) in subsection (2), for the words " The traffic commissioners " the words " A traffic commissioner " ; and

(*c*) in subsection (3), for the words " the traffic commissioner " the words " a traffic commissioner ".

(15) In section 55, for the word " commissioners " there shall be substituted the word " commissioner " and for the word " their " there shall be substituted the word " his ".

(16) In section 56, in subsection (1), there shall be substituted for the word " commissioners " the word " commissioner " and there shall be omitted the words " them or ".

(17) In section 57, for the word " commissioners ", whenever occurring, there shall be substituted the word " commissioner."

(18) In section 60(1), for the words " the commissioners " there shall be substituted the words " traffic commissioners ".

(19) In section 69(1), for the words " the traffic commissioners " there shall be substituted the words " a traffic commissioner ".

(20) In section 82 (interpretation), the following definition shall be inserted at the appropriate place—

" ' traffic commissioner ' means the person appointed to be the commissioner for a traffic area constituted for the purposes of this Act ; ".

(21) In Schedule 3 there shall be substituted—

    (*a*) in paragraph 1, for the words " traffic commissioners " in both places the words " a traffic commissioner " and for the word " commissioners ", in both places, the word " commissioner " ; and

    (*b*) in paragraphs 5 and 9, for the word " commissioners " whenever occurring the word " commissioner ".

The Civic Government (Scotland) Act 1982

5. In section 18 of the Civic Government (Scotland) Act 1982, there shall be substituted—

    (*a*) for the word " commissioners " whenever occurring the word " commissioner " ;

    (*b*) in subsection (2), for the word " them " the word " him " ;

    (*c*) in subsection (3), for the words " they consider " in both places the words " he considers ", for the words " they decided " the words " he decided " and for the words " they should consider " the words " he should consider " ;

    (*d*) in subsection (5), for the words " they alter " the words " he alters " ; and

    (*e*) in subsection (8), for the word " their " in both places the word " his ".

The Road Traffic Regulation Act 1984

6. In section 38(4) and (7) of and paragraph 31(*a*) of Schedule 9 to the Road Traffic Regulation Act 1984 there shall be substituted for the word " commissioners " in each place the word " commissioner ".

The London Regional Transport Act 1984

7. In Schedule 5 to the London Regional Transport Act 1984, there shall be substituted—

    (*a*) in paragraph 11(5), for the word " commissioners ", where it first occurs, the word " commissioner " and for the words " those commissioners " the words " the commissioner " ;

    (*b*) in paragraph 11(8), for the word " commissioners ", in both places, the word " commissioner " ; and

    (*c*) in paragraph 12(7), for the word " commissioners " the word " commissioner ".

SCHEDULE 3

Amendments Consequential on Section 57

The Transport Act 1968

1. The following provisions of the 1968 Act shall be omitted—

    section 17 (transfer to Executive of local authority transport undertakings) ;

section 18 (planning of passenger transport services in newly designated areas);

section 19 and Schedule 6 (provision for transfer of control of bus services in a designated area to the Executive for that area); and

section 21 (which contains provisions connected with those of section 19).

2. In—

(*a*) sections 10, 12, 14, 15, 20 and 23 of that Act; and

(*b*) paragraph 11(*a*) of Schedule 5 to that Act;

for the word " designated " (in each place where it occurs) there shall be substituted the words " passenger transport ".

3. In section 9(6) of that Act, the words " or 6 " shall be omitted, and for the words " sections 20(6) and (7) and 21(5) " there shall be substituted the words " section 20(6) and (7) ".

4. In section 10 of that Act (general powers of Executive)—

(*a*) in subsection (1)—

(i) in paragraph (ii) (power to carry passengers by land, otherwise than by road, and by water), for the words " the following distance " to the end of the paragraph there shall be substituted the words " the distance of twenty-five miles from the nearest point on the boundary of that area ; " ; and

(ii) in paragraph (xxiii), for the words " the discharge of their duty under section 9(3) of this Act " there shall be substituted the words " their business ; " ; and

(*b*) in subsection (2) (things done by subsidiaries to count as things done by Executive for certain purposes), the words from " or with the consent " to " Act " (which refer to consents under Schedule 6 to that Act) shall be omitted.

5. In section 11 of that Act (Executive's financial duty), as it applies to England and Wales, subsection (1) shall be omitted.

6. In section 12 of that Act (borrowing powers of Executive)—

(*a*) in subsection (3)(*d*) the words from " or by " to the end of the paragraph shall be omitted ; and

(*b*) in subsection (4)—

(i) for the words " Each of the councils of constituent areas " there shall be substituted the words " The Authority for the Executive's area " ;

(ii) for the words " such a council " there shall be substituted the words " the Authority for a passenger transport area " ; and

(iii) for the word " council " in each place where it occurs in paragraphs (*a*) and (*b*) there shall be substituted the word " Authority ".

7. For section 13 of that Act (precepting powers), as it applies to England and Wales, there shall be substituted the following section—

"Power to make grants. 13. The Authority shall have power to make grants to the Executive for any purpose."

8. In section 14(3) of that Act (accounts of Executive), as it applies to England and Wales, for the words " for the designated area and to each of the councils of constituent areas " there shall be substituted the words " and to each of the councils of the districts comprised in the county which is coterminous with or includes the Executive's area ".

9. In section 14(3) of that Act, as it applies to Scotland, the words " for the designated area " shall be omitted.

10.—(1) In section 15 of that Act (further functions of Authority)—

(*a*) subsection (1)(*a*) shall be omitted ;

(*b*) in subsection (2), in paragraph (*a*), the words from " or provided by " to " Act " shall be omitted ; and

(*c*) subsection (3) shall be omitted.

(2) In that section, as it applies to England and Wales—

(*a*) in subsection (2), the words following paragraph (*b*) ; and

(*b*) subsection (4) ;

shall be omitted.

(3) In subsection (2) of that section, as it applies to Scotland, the words from " and, in the case " to the end shall be omitted.

11. In section 15A of that Act (control of Executive by Authority) subsection (1) shall be omitted.

12. In section 16 of that Act (publication of annual report by Authority and Executive and prevention of improper conduct of subsidiary activities)—

(*a*) in subsection (1)—

(i) for the words " area designated by an order under section 9(1) of this Act " there shall be substituted the words " passenger transport area " ; and

(ii) for the words " by the order aforesaid " there shall be substituted the words " by any order made, or having effect as if made, under section 9(3) of this Act " ; and

(*b*) in subsection (2), the words from " and if " to " would not " shall be omitted.

13. In section 20 of that Act (special duty of Executive to enter into agreements with the Railways Board for securing necessary services)—

(*a*) in subsection (2)—

(i) for the words " general duty under section 9(3) "

there shall be substituted the words " duty under section 9A(3) " ;

(ii) the words " to which this section applies " shall be omitted ;

(iii) in paragraph (*a*), the words " review as soon as may be, and subsequently " shall be omitted ; and

(iv) in paragraph (*b*) (Executive to secure such railway passenger services as the Authority decide to be necessary to ensure a proper contribution towards provision of public passenger transport system required by section 9(1)), for the words from " decide " to the end there shall be substituted the words " consider it appropriate to secure to meet any public transport requirements within that area " ; and

(*b*) subsection (8) shall be omitted.

14. In section 22 of that Act (provisions as to orders and regulations under Part II)—

(*a*) in subsections (1) and (2) the words " or regulations " shall be omitted ; and

(*b*) subsections (3) to (6) shall be omitted.

15. In section 24(2) of that Act (co-operation between Passenger Transport Executives and the National Bus Company and the Scottish Transport Group), for the words from the beginning to " Act " there shall be substituted the words " In the case of any area which is a passenger transport area for the purposes of Part II of this Act ".

16. In section 54 of that Act (provisions with respect to railway closures)—

(*a*) in subsection (2), for the words " designated under section 9(1) thereof " there shall be substituted the words " which is a passenger transport area for the purposes of Part II of this Act " ; and

(*b*) in subsection (3), for the words " an area designated as aforesaid " there shall be substituted the words " any such area as is mentioned in that subsection ".

17. In section 134(1) of that Act (authorities to whom duty to act as a body engaged in a commercial enterprise applies), for the words from " designated " to " section 9(1) " there shall be substituted the words " area which is a passenger transport area for the purposes of Part II ".

18. In section 137 of that Act (obligation to establish machinery for negotiation and consultation with staff)—

(*a*) in subsection (1) (authorities to whom the section applies), for the words from " designated " to " section 9(1) " there shall be substituted the words " area which is a passenger transport area for the purposes of Part II " ;

(*b*) in subsection (3)(*b*), for the words from " Authority " to the end of the paragraph there shall be substituted the words

" Passenger Transport Authority for the passenger transport area in question (referred to below in this section as the relevant Passenger Transport Authority) " ; and

(c) in subsection (4), for the words " Authority established as aforesaid " and " Authority so established " there shall be substituted the words " relevant Passenger Transport Authority ".

19. In section 141(1) of that Act (application of Town and Country Planning Acts), for the words from " designated " to " section 9(1) " there shall be substituted the words " area which is a passenger transport area for the purposes of Part II ".

20. In section 160(5) of that Act (stamp duty not chargeable on certain instruments), for the words " established under section 9(1) " there shall be substituted the words " for any area which is a passenger transport area for the purposes of Part II ".

21.—(1) In Schedule 5 to that Act (constitution, etc., of Passenger Transport Authorities and Executives), Part I (which relates to Passenger Transport Authorities) shall be omitted.

(2) In Part II of that Schedule—

(a) paragraph 1 shall be omitted ;

(b) in paragraph 2, as it applies to England and Wales, for the words " any of the councils of constituent areas " (in each place where they occur) there shall be substituted the words " the Authority for the passenger transport area " ; and

(c) in paragraph 2, as it applies to Scotland, for the word " designated " there shall be substituted the words " passenger transport ".

(3) In Part III of that Schedule the following provisions shall be omitted—

(a) paragraphs 1, 2, 3(a), 4, 5, 10, 11(c), 12, 16 and 17 ;

(b) in paragraphs 6, 7 and 9 the words " the Authority and " and " respectively ", in each place where they occur ;

(c) in paragraph 8 the words " the Authority or " and " the chairman of the Authority or, as the case may be " ;

(d) in paragraph 11, the words " the Authority or " in sub-paragraph (a) and " the Authority " in sub-paragraph (b) ; and

(e) in paragraph 13, the words " the Authority or ", in both places where they occur, and " the Authority " where those words last occur ;

and in paragraph 3(b), for " 9(1)(b) " there shall be substituted " 9(2) ".

The Post Office Act 1969

22. In section 7(1A)(b) (bodies for whom the Post Office may perform services to include Passenger Transport Executives established under section 9(1)(b) of the 1968 Act), for the words " established under section 9(1)(b) " there shall be substituted the words " for the purposes of Part II ".

The Pensions (Increase) Act 1971

23. In paragraph 6(2)(c) of Schedule 3 to the Pensions (Increase) Act 1971 (extended definition of employing authority), for the words from " established under section 9(1) " to the end there shall be substituted the words " for the purposes of Part II of the Transport Act 1968 "

1968 c. 73.

1972 c. 70.

The Local Government Act 1972

24. In section 202 of the 1972 Act (public transport in passenger transport areas) subsections (1) and (3) to (7) shall be omitted.

25. In Schedule 24 to that Act, Part II shall be omitted.

1973 c. 65.

The Local Government (Scotland) Act 1973

26. In section 150 of the Local Government (Scotland) Act 1973, subsection (5) shall be omitted.

27. Section 151 of that Act shall be omitted.

28. In Schedule 18 to that Act, paragraphs 1(a) to (d) and (f), 7(c), 10, 11 and 21(1) shall be omitted.

1980 c. 65.

The Local Government, Planning and Land Act 1980

29. In section 82 of the Local Government, Planning and Land Act 1980 (Passenger Transport Executives and their subsidiaries)—

    (a) in subsection (1)—

        (i) in paragraph (a) the words " whose area is either the whole or part of one county " shall be omitted, and for the words " county council " there shall be substituted the words " metropolitan county passenger transport authority for the county which is coterminous with or includes that Executive's area " ; and

        (ii) for the word " council " in each place where it occurs in paragraphs (b) to (d) there shall be substituted the word " authority " ;

    (b) subsections (2) and (3) shall be omitted ; and

    (c) in subsection (4), for the words " subsections (1) to (3) " there shall be substituted the words " subsection (1) ".

1983 c. 10.

The Transport Act 1983

30. In section 1 of the Transport Act 1983 (interpretation of Part I), in paragraph (a) of the definition of " Executive ", for the words from " an area " to " county " there shall be substituted the words " any passenger transport area (within the meaning of Part II of the Act of 1968) ".

31. In section 3(3) of that Act (formulation of Executive's financial plan may assume grants will be provided by the Authority to extent considered necessary by the Executive for discharge of certain duties), for the words " general duty under section 9(3) " there shall be substituted the words " duty under section 9A(3) ".

32. In section 9 of that Act (repeals and minor amendments), subsection (2) shall be omitted.

The Road Traffic Regulation Act 1984

33. In paragraph 31(*b*) of Schedule 9 to the Road Traffic Regulation Act 1984 (local authority to consult Passenger Transport Executive before making certain orders) for the words from " designated under section 9(1)" to the end there shall be substituted the words "which is a passenger transport area for the purposes of Part II of the Transport Act 1968, shall consult with the Passenger Transport Executive for that passenger transport area.".

SCHEDULE 4

Constitution, Powers and Proceedings of the Transport Tribunal

Constitution

1. The Transport Tribunal shall be a court of record and have an official seal which shall be judicially noticed.

2.—(1) The tribunal shall consist of—

    (*a*) a president and two or more chairmen appointed by the Lord Chancellor (referred to below in this Schedule as judicial members) ; and

    (*b*) two or more other members appointed by the Secretary of State.

(2) The president of the tribunal shall be a barrister, advocate or solicitor of not less than ten years' standing, and each chairman shall be a barrister, advocate or solicitor of not less than seven years' standing.

Tenure of Office

3.—(1) Subject to the following provisions of this paragraph, each judicial member of the tribunal shall hold office until the end of the completed year of service in which he reaches the age of seventy-two and shall then retire.

(2) Where the Lord Chancellor considers it desirable in the public interest to retain a judicial member in office after he reaches that age, he may from time to time authorise that member's continuance in office until such date (not later than the date on which that member reaches seventy-five) as he thinks fit.

(3) The Lord Chancellor may, if he thinks fit, remove a judicial member from office on the ground of incapacity or misbehaviour.

(4) A judicial member may at any time by notice in writing to the Lord Chancellor resign his office.

(5) Subject to the preceding provisions of this paragraph and to paragraph 6 below, a judicial member shall hold and vacate office in accordance with such terms and conditions as may be determined by the Lord Chancellor at the time of his appointment and shall, on ceasing to hold office, be eligible for reappointment.

4.—(1) A member of the tribunal appointed by the Secretary of State shall hold and vacate office in accordance with such terms and conditions (both as to his term of office and otherwise) as may be determined by the Secretary of State at the time of his appointment and, on ceasing to hold office, be eligible (subject to the following provisions of this paragraph) for reappointment.

(2) Subject to sub-paragraph (3) below, a person shall not be appointed as a member of the tribunal by the Secretary of State for a term extending beyond the end of the completed year of service in which he reaches seventy.

(3) Where the Secretary of State considers it desirable in the public interest that a person should be appointed for a term exceeding that allowed under sub-paragraph (2) above, that person may be appointed for such term, not extending beyond the date on which he reaches seventy-five, as the Secretary of State thinks fit.

(4) A member appointed by the Secretary of State may at any time by notice in writing to the Secretary of State resign his office.

Staff of the tribunal

5. The Secretary of State may make available to the tribunal such staff as he considers necessary for assisting the tribunal in the proper execution of their duties.

Remuneration and expenses

6. There shall be paid to the members of the tribunal such remuneration as the Secretary of State may with the consent of the Treasury determine.

7. Any remuneration payable under paragraph 6 above and any other expenses of the tribunal shall be met by the Secretary of State.

Powers and proceedings

8.—(1) Subject to paragraph 9(2) below, the tribunal shall for the purpose of the exercise of any of their functions have full jurisdiction to hear and determine all matters whether of law or of fact.

(2) As respects—

(a) the attendance and examination of witnesses ;

(b) the production and inspection of documents ;

(c) the enforcement of their orders ;

(d) the entry on and inspection of property ; and

(e) other matters necessary or proper for the due exercise of their jurisdiction ;

the tribunal shall have, in England and Wales, all such powers, rights and privileges as are vested in the High Court, and, in Scotland, all such powers, rights and privileges as are vested in the Court of Session.

(3) Execution may be had in England and Wales of any order of the tribunal as if it were an order of the High Court, and any order of the tribunal may be recorded for execution in the books of council and session in Scotland, and shall be enforceable accordingly.

9.—(1) On an appeal from any determination of a traffic commissioner under Part V of the 1968 Act, the 1981 Act or this Act, the tribunal shall have power—

    (*a*) to make such order as they think fit ; or

    (*b*) to remit the matter to the traffic commissioner for rehearing and determination by him in any case where they consider it appropriate ;

and any such order shall be binding on the traffic commissioner.

(2) The tribunal may not on any such appeal take into consideration any circumstances which did not exist at the time of the determination which is the subject of the appeal.

10.—(1) The president or, in his absence, such one of the other judicial members as the president or (if the president is unable for any reason to exercise the power conferred on him by this subparagraph) the Secretary of State may direct, shall preside at any sitting of the tribunal.

(2) The president or other judicial member presiding at a sitting of the tribunal in pursuance of sub-paragraph (1) above is referred to below in this paragraph as the presiding member.

(3) If at any sitting of the tribunal the members sitting are evenly divided as to any decision, the presiding member shall have a second or casting vote ; but otherwise decisions of the tribunal shall be by a majority of the members sitting.

11.—(1) Subject to paragraph 10 above, the Secretary of State may from time to time make general rules governing the procedure and practice of the tribunal and generally for carrying into effect the tribunal's duties and powers.

(2) Without prejudice to the generality of sub-paragraph (1) above, rules under that sub-paragraph may provide for—

    (*a*) the awarding of costs by the tribunal ;

    (*b*) the reference of any question to a member of the tribunal, or to any other person appointed by them, for report after holding a local inquiry ;

    (*c*) the review by the tribunal of decisions previously given by them ;

I

(*d*) the number of members of the tribunal to constitute a quorum ;

(*e*) enabling the tribunal to dispose of any proceedings notwithstanding that in the course of those proceedings there has been a change in the persons sitting as members of the tribunal ; and

(*f*) the right of audience before the tribunal.

(3) Rules under sub-paragraph (1) above may also, subject to the consent of the Treasury, prescribe the scale of fees for and in connection with proceedings before the tribunal.

12.—(1) The Secretary of State shall give to the tribunal such assistance as the tribunal may reasonably require.

(2) The Secretary of State shall place at the disposal of the tribunal any information in his possession which he considers will be of assistance to the tribunal in connection with any matter before them, and shall be entitled to appear and be heard in any proceedings before the tribunal.

13.—(1) Subject to sub-paragraph (2) below and to any rules made under paragraph 11 above, the tribunal may sit in any part of Great Britain in such place or places as may be convenient for the determination of the proceedings before them.

(2) An appeal from the determination of a traffic commissioner for a traffic area in Scotland shall be heard in Scotland.

Appeals

14.—(1) Subject to sub-paragraphs (2) and (3) below, an appeal shall lie in accordance with rules made by the Secretary of State from the tribunal to the Court of Appeal or to the Court of Session.

(2) No appeal shall lie from the tribunal upon a question of fact or locus standi.

(3) An appeal shall not be brought except in conformity with such rules of court as may from time to time be made in relation to such appeals by the authority having power to make rules of court for the Court of Appeal or the Court of Session (as the case may be).

(4) On the hearing of an appeal the Court of Appeal and the Court of Session may draw all such inferences as are not inconsistent with the facts expressly found and are necessary for determining the question of law, and may make any order which the tribunal could have made, and also any such further or other order as may be just.

(5) The costs of and incidental to an appeal shall be at the discretion of the Court, but neither the tribunal nor any member of the tribunal shall be liable to any costs by reason or in respect of any appeal.

(6) Subject to sub-paragraph (7) below, the decision of the Court of Appeal or the Court of Session (as the case may be) shall be final.

(7) Where there has been a difference of opinion between those Courts, either of those Courts in which a matter affected by such a

difference of opinion is pending may give leave to appeal to the House of Lords on such terms as to costs as that Court shall determine.

Exercise of powers by Lord Chancellor

15. The Lord Chancellor shall consult the Lord Advocate before exercising any of his powers under this Schedule.

Annual report

16. The tribunal shall make annually a report of all their proceedings to the Secretary of State and it shall be laid before Parliament.

SCHEDULE 5

THE DISABLED PERSONS TRANSPORT ADVISORY COMMITTEE

Administration, etc.

1. The Secretary of State shall make arrangements for the Committee to be provided with such administrative support and office accommodation as he considers appropriate.

2. The Secretary of State shall provide the Committee with funds with which to pay to their members such travelling and other allowances, and to defray such other expenses in connection with their functions, as he may determine.

Constitution and procedure

3.—(1) Any person appointed to be a member of the Committee shall hold and vacate office in accordance with the terms of his appointment and shall, on ceasing to be a member of the Committee, be eligible for re-appointment.

(2) Any person so appointed may at any time resign his office by written notice given to the Secretary of State.

4.—(1) The Committee shall meet whenever convened by the chairman and at least four times a year.

(2) Without prejudice to the discretion of the chairman to call a meeting whenever he thinks fit, he shall call one when required to do so by any five members of the Committee.

(3) Minutes shall be kept of the proceedings of every meeting of the Committee.

(4) Subject to the preceding provisions of this paragraph, the Committee shall determine their own procedure (including the quorum at their meetings).

5. The Committee may delegate the exercise and performance of any of their functions to such of their sub-committees as they think fit.

6. The validity of any proceedings of the Committee shall not be affected by any vacancy amongst the members, by any defect in the appointment of a member or by any failure to comply with the requirement imposed by section 125(3) of this Act.

SCHEDULE 6

TRANSITIONAL PROVISIONS AND SAVINGS

Road service licensing during transitional period

1.—(1) In this paragraph " the transitional period " means the period beginning with the day on which this paragraph is brought into force and ending with 25th October 1986.

(2) During the transitional period, Part III of the 1981 Act shall apply in relation to services which do not involve the use of any place in London as a stopping place with the modifications set out in paragraphs 2 to 5 below.

2.—(1) In paragraphs (*a*) and (*b*) of section 31(2) for the words " be against the interests of the public " there shall, in each case, be substituted the words " interfere with the transition to deregulation ".

(2) For subsections (3) and (4) of section 31 there shall be substituted the following subsections—

" (3) For the purposes of subsection (1) above the grant of a road service licence shall be taken to interfere with the transition to deregulation if, but only if—

(*a*) it has a severely detrimental effect on traffic conditions ;

(*b*) it disrupts arrangements made, or proposed to be made—

(i) in England and Wales, by a non-metropolitan county council or Passenger Transport Executive ; and

(ii) in Scotland, by a regional or islands council or Passenger Transport Executive ;

with a view to achieving a satisfactory transition to deregulation ; or

(*c*) the applicant is in receipt of a subsidy from one or more local authorities otherwise than—

(i) under an agreement with respect to which the requirements of section 89 of the Transport Act 1985 are satisfied ; or

(ii) by way of reimbursement for providing travel concessions in accordance with a travel concession scheme which satisfies the requirements of section 93 of that Act ;

and that subsidy gives the applicant an unfair commercial advantage in relation to the provision of any local service in the area in question ;

and in this Part of this Act references to " interference with the transition to deregulation " shall be construed accordingly.

(4) In considering whether the grant of a licence would interfere with the transition to deregulation, the commissioners—

(*a*) shall have regard to any objections or other representations (made to them in the prescribed manner) which they consider are relevant ; and

(*b*) shall not consider whether the grant would be dis-
ruptive as mentioned in subsection (3)(*b*) above except
at the instance of the council or Executive concerned."

(3) In subsection (5), after the words " police district " there shall
be inserted the words " and Passenger Transport Executive for
any area ".

3.—(1) In section 32 (attachment to licences of conditions as to
matters other than fares)—

(*a*) in subsection (1), for the words from " interests of the
public " to " Act " there shall be substituted the words
" desirability of preventing interference with the transition
to deregulation " ;

(*b*) in subsection (3)—

(i) in paragraph (*a*), for the words " interests of the
public " there shall be substituted the words " desirability
of preventing interference with the transition to deregulation " ; and

(ii) in paragraphs (*b*) and (*c*), for the words " those
interests " there shall, in each case, be substituted " that
desirability " ; and

(*c*) in subsections (4) and (5) for the words from " be against "
to the end there shall be substituted, in each case, the
words " interfere with the transition to deregulation ".

4. In section 34 (grant of road service licences for services on
routes not otherwise served), in subsection (1)(*a*) for the words from
" be against " to " public " there shall be substituted the words
" interfere with the transition to deregulation ", and subsection (1)(*b*)
shall apply with the necessary modifications.

5. In section 50(8) (persons who, in addition to applicant, have
right of appeal against decision of traffic commissioners), in paragraph (*a*), after the words " local authority " there shall be inserted
the words " or Passenger Transport Executive ".

Registration of local services outside London

6.—(1) In paragraphs 7 to 12 below—

" local service " means a local service which is not a London
local service ;

" relevant authority ", in relation to a local service, means any
Passenger Transport Executive or non-metropolitan county,
regional or islands council within whose area there will be a
stopping place for the service ;

" road service licence " has the same meaning as in the 1981
Act ; and

" the transitional period " has the same meaning as in paragraph 1 of this Schedule.

(2) Section 135(3) of this Act shall not apply to any regulations
made under paragraphs 7 to 11 below.

SCH. 6

(3) For the purposes of paragraph 8 below, a local service is improved if, but only if, there is any increase in—

(a) the frequency of the service ;

(b) the length of its route ;

(c) the number of stopping places for the service ; or

(d) the number of passengers which can be carried by the service taken as a whole.

7.—(1) Where an application for registration of the prescribed particulars of a local service falls within one of the Cases mentioned in sub-paragraph (2) below—

(a) the traffic commissioner to whom the application is made shall register those particulars ;

(b) they shall be deemed to have been registered with him under section 6 of this Act ; and

(c) the period of notice (mentioned in section 6) in relation to that registration shall be deemed to have expired.

(2) The Cases are—

CASE A

Where—

(a) the application for registration of the prescribed particulars of a local service is received by the traffic commissioner at any time before 1st March 1986 ; and

(b) the prescribed requirements are satisfied in relation to the application.

CASE B

Where—

(a) the application for registration of the prescribed particulars of a local service is received by the traffic commissioner at any time after the grant of the licence mentioned in paragraph (b) below but before 14th September 1986 ;

(b) a road service licence has been granted for that service at any time after 28th February 1986 ; and

(c) the prescribed requirements are satisfied in relation to the application.

CASE C

Where—

(a) the application for registration of the prescribed particulars of a local service is received by the traffic commissioner at any time during the period beginning with 1st March 1986 and ending with 13th September 1986 ;

(b) the particulars of the service are the same as those of a trial area service ; and

(c) the prescribed requirements are satisfied in relation to the application.

In this Case " trial area service " means a local service provided in a trial area (as defined by section 38 of the 1981 Act) and in respect of which the requirements of section 40 of that Act (duty to publish particulars of services in trial areas) have been satisfied.

CASE D

Where—

(a) the application for registration of the prescribed particulars of a local service is received by the traffic commissioner at any time during the period beginning with 1st March 1986 and ending with 25th October 1986 ;

(b) the application is supported in writing, in accordance with sub-paragraph (3) below, by an authority responsible for expenditure on public passenger transport services (as defined for Part V of this Act by section 88(8)) ; and

(c) the prescribed requirements are satisfied in relation to the application.

(3) An authority of the kind mentioned in paragraph (b) of Case D shall give their support to an application in accordance with this sub-paragraph if, but only if, the local service in question is one—

(a) which the operator has contracted with that authority to operate under an agreement providing for service subsidies ; or

(b) for the provision of which that authority have issued an invitation to tender under section 89 of this Act and for which the person applying for registration of the particulars of the service has submitted a tender to provide the service without subsidy ; or

(c) in respect of which the conditions mentioned in sub-paragraph (4) below are satisfied.

(4) The conditions are that—

(a) the service is to be operated by a person who has entered into an agreement with London Regional Transport (" LRT ") to operate it ; and

(b) the authority has entered into an agreement or arrangement with LRT to contribute to the costs incurred by LRT in securing the service.

Variation and cancellation of registrations during transitional period

8.—(1) Where the prescribed particulars of a local service have been registered with a traffic commissioner under paragraph 7 above and an application is made to him for the variation or cancellation of the registration, he shall vary or (as the case may be) cancel the registration if he is satisfied that the application falls within one of the Cases mentioned in sub-paragraph (2) below.

(2) The Cases are—

CASE 1

Where—

(a) the application is made by the operator of the service to which the registration relates ;

(b) the application is received by the traffic commissioner at any time before 1st March 1986 ; and (*c*) the prescribed requirements are satisfied in relation to the application.

CASE 2

Where—

(*a*) the application is made by the operator of the service to which the registration relates ;

(*b*) the application is received by the traffic commissioner at any time during the period beginning with 1st March 1986 and ending with 31st July 1986 ;

(*c*) the application is supported in writing, in accordance with sub-paragraph (3) below, by each relevant authority ; and

(*d*) in the case of an application for variation, a service operated in accordance with the particulars as proposed to be varied would not amount to a service improved by comparison with a service operated in accordance with the particulars as registered.

Where a relevant authority have refused to support the application but the traffic commissioner is of the opinion that no such authority acting reasonably would have refused to support it he may, at the request of the applicant, proceed as if paragraph (*c*) of this Case were omitted.

CASE 3

Where the application—

(*a*) is for the variation of the registered particulars ;

(*b*) is made by the operator of the service to which the registration relates ;

(*c*) is received by the traffic commissioner at any time during the period beginning with 1st March 1986 and ending with 25th October 1986 ; and

(*d*) is supported in writing, in accordance with sub-paragraph (4) below, by each relevant authority.

(3) Where a relevant authority are asked by the operator of a local service to provide written support, in accordance with this sub-paragraph, for an application for the variation or cancellation of the registration of the prescribed particulars of the service, the authority shall do so if, but only if, they are satisfied—

(*a*) that any demand which would have been met by a service operated in accordance with the registered particulars would be met—

(i) by a service operated in accordance with the particulars as proposed to be varied ; or

(ii) by another service the particulars of which have been registered under paragraph 7 above ; or

(*b*) that there has been a change of circumstances—

(i) which seriously impairs the ability of the operator of the service to operate it in accordance with the registered particulars ; and

(ii) which could not reasonably have been foreseen by
him.

(4) Where a relevant authority are asked by the operator of a
local service to provide written support, in accordance with this
sub-paragraph, for an application for the variation of the registration of the prescribed particulars of the service, the authority may
do so if they are satisfied—

    (*a*) that a variation of the particulars of the service is desirable
in the interests of producing a pattern of service which
is better suited to meeting the public transport requirements of their area ; and

    (*b*) where a service operated in accordance with the particu-
lars as proposed to be varied would amount to a service
improved by comparison with a service operated in accordance with the particulars as registered, that any demand
met by the improvement to the service could not be met
by any other local service if the improvement were not
made.

Duty to notify relevant authorities of applications for registrations etc.

9.—(1) Any person making an application which falls within
one of the Cases mentioned in paragraph 7 above shall—

    (*a*) notify each relevant authority of the application and of the
particulars to be registered ; and

    (*b*) furnish each such authority with such further information
as may be prescribed.

(2) Any person making an application which falls within one
of the Cases mentioned in paragraph 8 above shall—

    (*a*) notify each relevant authority of the application and, in
the case of an application for the variation of registered
particulars, of the variation to be registered ; and

    (*b*) furnish each such authority with such further information
as may be prescribed.

Publication of information by traffic commissioner

10.—(1) Each traffic commissioner shall publish such information
with respect to applications made to him under any of the Cases
mentioned in paragraphs 7 and 8 above as may be prescribed.

(2) Information with respect to applications falling within Case
A in paragraph 7 above, or Case 1 in paragraph 8 above, shall
be published—

    (*a*) separately from the other information which is required to be
published by sub-paragraph (1) above ; and

    (*b*) before 1st April 1986.

(3) Where a traffic commissioner is required by sub-paragraph
(1) above to publish any information, he shall give that information to any Passenger Transport Executive, district council in
England and Wales or county, regional or islands council in whose
area lies any part of the route of the service.

School buses

11.—(1) For the purpose of ensuring that in the school year beginning in 1986 satisfactory provision can be made for transporting those pupils for whom a local education authority (or, in Scotland, an education authority) are under a duty to provide transport, the Secretary of State may by regulations make provision (including provision modifying this Schedule) for enabling approved local services to be operated during the transitional period without road service licences.

(2) In this paragraph " approved ", in relation to a local service, means approved by the traffic commissioner for the traffic area in which the service is to be provided.

Continuation of existing road service licences

12. A road service licence (other than one for a service with no stopping place outside London) which is in force when this Act is passed but which would otherwise expire before 25th October 1986 shall, unless previously revoked, continue in force to the end of that day.

In the application of this paragraph section 34(3) of this Act shall be disregarded.

Traffic commissioners

13.—(1) The person who, immediately before the commencement of section 3 of this Act, was the chairman of the traffic commissioners for any traffic area shall be deemed to have been appointed by the Secretary of State (under section 4 of the 1981 Act as substituted by section 3 of this Act) as the traffic commissioner for that area on the same terms and conditions as those on which he was appointed as chairman of the traffic commissioners ; and in relation to any such person appointed before 1st May 1985, subsection (4)(b) of the substituted section 4 shall have effect as if for the words from " sixty-five " to " direct " there were substituted the word " seventy ".

(2) For the purposes of the principal civil service pension scheme any period of service as chairman of the traffic commissioners for any area which ends with the commencement of section 3 of this Act and any period of service as traffic commissioner for that area which begins on that commencement shall be treated as a single, unbroken, period of service.

PSV operators' licences

14.—(1) This paragraph applies where the condition attached under section 16(1) of the 1981 Act (maximum number of vehicles which may be used) to a restricted PSV operator's licence in force at the commencement of section 24 of this Act specifies more than two vehicles as the maximum.

(2) The traffic commissioner for the traffic area in question shall, for the purpose of securing that the licence complies with section 16(1A) of that Act, vary the condition but shall direct that the variation of the condition shall not take effect before the end of such period as appears to him to be reasonably required to enable the

holder of the licence to make arrangements to comply with the Sch. 6 condition as varied.

Appeals under section 18 of Civic Government (Scotland) Act 1982 (c.45)

15. Anything done or treated by virtue of any enactment as having been done under section 18 of the Civic Government (Scotland) Act 1982 before the coming into force of paragraph 5 of Part II of Schedule 2 to this Act which could be done under the said section 18 as amended by the said paragraph shall be treated as having been done under the said section 18 as so amended.

London local service licences

16.—(1) A road service licence which—

(a) is in force immediately before section 35 of this Act comes into force ; and

(b) applies to a service which on the coming into force of section 35 is a London local service ;

shall be treated for the purposes of this Act as a London local service licence granted under Part II (and, if granted under section 35 or 35A of the 1981 Act, as granted under section 39 of this Act).

(2) Subject to sub-paragraph (3) below, the terms and conditions applicable to any such licence shall be those applicable to it immediately before section 35 of this Act comes into force.

(3) Section 41 of this Act shall apply to any such licence as if it had been granted for a period ending with the date on which it would have expired under section 37 of the 1981 Act ; and any condition attached to the licence under section 33 of that Act (conditions as to fares) shall cease to have effect.

(4) In this paragraph and paragraph 17 below " road service licence " means a road service licence under Part III of the 1981 Act.

17. In relation to a London local service—

(a) any application for a road service licence in respect of that service made under section 31 of the 1981 Act and not determined before the date on which section 35 of this Act comes into force shall be treated as an application for a London local service licence made under section 37 of this Act ;

(b) any decision of the metropolitan traffic commissioners or (as the case may be) of the Secretary of State under any provision of the 1981 Act with respect to—

(i) the grant, revocation or suspension of a road service licence in respect of that service ; or

(ii) the attachment of any condition to such a road service licence or the variation or renewal of any condition attached to such a road service licence ;

SCH. 6

shall be treated as made in relation to a London local service licence in respect of that service by the metropolitan traffic commissioner or (as the case may be) by the Secretary of State under the corresponding provision of Part II of this Act ; and

(c) any appeal or other proceeding pending under the 1981 Act with respect to any such decision may be proceeded with under the corresponding provision of Part II of this Act.

18. In so far as any regulations in force immediately before sections 31 and 42 of this Act come into force then have effect as if made under section 50(9) of the 1981 Act (procedure on appeals under that section) with respect to appeals under any of the provisions of subsections (1) to (5) and (7) of that section, those regulations shall have effect as if made under section 42(10) of this Act with respect to appeals under the corresponding provision of that section.

Compensation for loss of employment, etc.

19. Any regulations made under section 17(3) of the 1968 Act which are in force immediately before the repeal of that section by this Act—

(a) shall continue in force notwithstanding that repeal ; and

(b) may be varied or revoked by regulations made under section 84 of this Act as if they had been made by reason of any such transfer of property, rights and liabilities as is mentioned in section 84(1)(c).

Tendering

20.—(1) Section 89 of this Act shall not apply in relation to any agreement providing for service subsidies entered into by an authority responsible for expenditure on public passenger transport services during the transitional period if none of the service subsidies under the agreement is payable in respect of the provision after the end of that period of any public passenger transport service.

(2) Sub-paragraph (1) above shall be read as if contained in Part V of this Act.

(3) In this paragraph " the transitional period " means the period beginning with the day on which section 89 of this Act comes into force and ending with 25th October 1986.

1978 c. 55.   *Agreements under section 3 of the Transport Act 1978*

21.—(1) Where—

(a) before the date on which the repeal by this Act of section 3 of the Transport Act 1978 comes into force any non-metropolitan county council have, in exercise of the power conferred by that section, entered into an agreement with London Regional Transport under which payments fall to be made by that council towards expenses incurred by

London Regional Transport in securing the provision of a   Sch. 6
public passenger transport service (" the old agreement ") ;

(*b*) the service is provided under an agreement entered into by
London Regional Transport accepting a tender invited for its
provision ; and

(*c*) the old agreement is still in force immediately before that
date ;

that council shall have power to enter into a new agreement with
London Regional Transport to contribute towards any of the expenses
to which they were liable to contribute in respect of that service under
the old agreement.

(2) An agreement entered into under this paragraph shall be made
so as to remain in force for a period ending not later than the date
on which the agreement mentioned in sub-paragraph (1)(*b*) above
expires.

Travel concessions

22.—(1) A scheme established under section 93 of this Act shall
not come into operation before 26th October 1986.

(2) The authority or authorities responsible for administration of
any scheme under that section shall not have power under section
97(2) of this Act to serve on any person for the purposes of that
scheme a participation notice which has an operative date falling
before 1st April 1987 unless the relevant publication date in relation
to that scheme falls before 8th April 1986.

(3) For the purposes of sub-paragraph (2) above—

(*a*) the operative date of a participation notice shall be taken to
be the date immediately following the end of such period
of notice as may be specified in the participation notice for
the purposes of section 97(5)(*a*) of this Act ; and

(*b*) the relevant publication date in relation to any such scheme
is the date (or whichever last occurs of the respective dates)
of first publication under section 95 of this Act of particulars
of the scheme and of the current reimbursement arrangements for eligible service operators participating in the
scheme as they are to apply on initial establishment of the
scheme.

(4) Expressions used in this paragraph to which a meaning is
given for any purposes of Part V of this Act have the same meaning
in this paragraph.

23.—(1) Notwithstanding the repeal by this Act of the Travel
Concessions Acts 1955 and 1964, section 138 of the 1968 Act and
section 1(1) of the Concessionary Travel for Handicapped Persons 1980 c. 29.
(Scotland) Act 1980, but subject to the following provisions of this
paragraph—

(*a*) the Acts of 1955 and 1964 and section 1(1) of the Act of
1980 shall continue to have effect in relation to any council
of any description within section 66(1) of this Act who—

(i) at the time when section 66 comes into force are
providing a service for the carriage of passengers by road
which requires a PSV operator's licence ; and

(ii) immediately before the date on which that repeal comes into force are granting travel concessions under arrangements made under the Acts of 1955 and 1964 or (as the case may be) under section 1(1) of the Act of 1980 to persons travelling on any such service operated by them ;

so long as the council retain their bus operating powers and continue to provide that service ; and

(*b*) section 138(2) of the 1968 Act shall continue to have effect for the purpose of authorising any local authority who immediately before that date are contributing to the cost incurred by that council in granting those concessions to continue to do so.

(2) Subject to the following provisions of this paragraph, where in the case of any such council—

(*a*) any such arrangements ("the former arrangements") are in force immediately before the date on which any scheme or order under Part IV of this Act providing for the transfer to any company or companies of property, rights and liabilities comprised in that council's bus undertaking comes into force ; and

(*b*) that council retain their bus operating powers during any period after that date ;

the council may reimburse the cost incurred by any company to which any public service vehicles formerly used or appropriated for use for the purposes of the council's bus undertaking are transferred under the scheme or order in granting travel concessions at any time during that period in accordance with arrangements made with that company ("the new arrangements") which meet the requirements of sub-paragraph (3) below.

(3) Subject to the following provisions of this paragraph, the travel concessions to be granted under the new arrangements—

(*a*) shall correspond to the travel concessions available under the former arrangements ; and

(*b*) shall be available in respect of journeys on public service vehicles transferred to the company in question under the scheme or order and used in operating services on routes to which the former arrangements applied.

(4) In any case to which sub-paragraph (2) above applies any local authority who immediately before the date on which the scheme or order in question comes into force are contributing to the cost incurred by the council in question in granting travel concessions under the former arrangements may contribute to any cost incurred by that council under sub-paragraph (2) above.

(5) Sub-paragraph (1) above, and sub-paragraph (2) above so far as relates to travel concessions granted on or after the date on which the repeal mentioned in sub-paragraph (1) above comes into force—

(*a*) shall not apply in relation to any council unless there is in operation on that date a scheme established under section 93 of this Act by that council, or by authorities who include that council, which covers the whole of that council's area ; and

(b) where any such scheme which is in operation on that date subsequently ceases to operate, shall not apply in relation to the granting of travel concessions or (as the case may be) in relation to travel concessions granted at any time after the date on which the scheme ceases to operate.

(6) The travel concessions—

(a) that may be provided under the Acts of 1955 and 1964 or (as the case may be) under the Act of 1980 by virtue of sub-paragraph (1) above ; and

(b) that may be financed by any council under sub-paragraph (2) above ;

shall be limited to concessions which correspond to travel concessions available at the time in question under the scheme mentioned in sub-paragraph (5) above.

(7) For the purposes of sub-paragraph (3)(a) or (as the case may be) sub-paragraph (6) above, travel concessions correspond to any other travel concessions in question if they are—

(a) of the same value ;

(b) available subject to the same terms, limitations or conditions : and

(c) available to persons of the same descriptions ;

as those other concessions.

(8) A council of any description within section 66(1) of this Act who at the time when that section comes into force are providing a service for the carriage of passengers by road which requires a PSV operator's licence shall be regarded for the purposes of this paragraph as retaining their bus operating powers until section 66(1) has effect in relation to that council.

(9) In this paragraph "local authority" has the same meaning as in section 93 of this Act, and expressions to which a meaning is given for any purposes of Part IV or Part V of this Act have the same meaning.

24. During any period after section 104 of this Act comes into force and before the repeal by this Act of section 138 of the 1968 Act comes into force section 15(2)(b) of that Act (approval of Passenger Transport Authority required for reduction or waiver of charges by Executive) shall have effect as if the reference to section 104(2) of this Act (substituted by paragraph 8 of Schedule 7 to this Act for a reference to section 138(1) of that Act) included a reference to section 138(1) of that Act.

The Transport Tribunal

25.—(1) The repeals made by this Act which relate to the Transport Tribunal shall not affect any judgment or order given, any document issued or any other thing done under any repealed enact-

Sch. 6 ment before the date on which the repeals take effect; and any such judgment or order, document or thing shall have effect as if it had been given, issued or (as the case may be) done under the provision of this Act corresponding to the repealed enactment.

(2) Any reference in any instrument or other document to such an enactment shall be taken as regards anything done after that date as a reference to the corresponding provision of this Act.

(3) Without prejudice to the generality of sub-paragraph (1) above, any rules made by the Transport Tribunal under paragraph 11 of Schedule 10 to the 1962 Act which are in operation immediately before Schedule 4 to this Act comes into force shall have effect as if they had been made by the Secretary of State under paragraph 11 of Schedule 4.

(4) Sub-paragraph (1) above does not apply in relation to any appointment made under Schedule 10 to the 1962 Act.

(5) Paragraphs 3 and 4(1) of Schedule 10 to the 1962 Act (appointment of members of the tribunal and tenure of office of the president) shall continue to apply in relation to the person who, at the time when section 117 of this Act comes into force, is the president of the Transport Tribunal, notwithstanding their repeal by this Act; and Schedule 4 to this Act shall have effect, so far as relates to the appointment and tenure of office of the president of the tribunal, subject to the provisions of this sub-paragraph.

(6) Any person who, immediately before section 117 of this Act comes into force, is a member of the special panel mentioned in subsection (3)(*a*) of that section, shall be treated as if he had been appointed by the Lord Chancellor, on the coming into force of that section, as a chairman of the Transport Tribunal under paragraph 2(1)(*a*) of Schedule 4 to this Act.

(7) Sub-paragraph (6) above applies in relation to any such person whether or not he would be qualified for such appointment in accordance with paragraph 2(2) of that Schedule; and, subject to paragraphs 3 and 6 of that Schedule, the terms and conditions applicable to any such person's tenure of office as such a chairman shall be the same as those applicable to his office immediately before section 117 of this Act comes into force.

(8) Any person other than the president of the Transport Tribunal who is a member of the tribunal at the time when that section comes into force shall be treated as if he had been appointed as such a member by the Secretary of State under paragraph 2(1)(*b*) of Schedule 4 to this Act for a term ending when his current term of office expires, and otherwise on the same terms and conditions as those applicable to his office immediately before that section comes into force.

(9) Rules made by the Secretary of State under paragraph 11 of Schedule 4 to this Act may include provision for applying those rules to proceedings pending before the tribunal at the time when those rules come into force with any modifications which appear to the Secretary of State to be necessary or desirable.

Transfers under section 17 of the 1968 Act

26. Notwithstanding the repeal by this Act of—

    (*a*) section 17 of the 1968 Act (transfer to Executive of local authority transport undertakings) ; and

    (*b*) section 202(4) of the 1972 Act (power by order establishing Passenger Transport Executive to make any provision that could be made by an order under section 17 of the 1968 Act) ;

the provisions of Schedule 4 to the 1968 Act, as they had effect immediately before that repeal came into operation, continue to apply for the purpose of determining the effect or giving effect to, or making any provision consequential on or incidental to, any transfer under section 17 (including that section as applied by section 202(4)).

SCHEDULE 7

Minor and Consequential Amendments

General

1. In England and Wales, the provisions made by or under any enactment which apply to motor vehicles used—

    (*a*) to carry passengers under a contract express or implied for the use of the vehicle as a whole at or for a fixed or agreed rate or sum ; and

    (*b*) to ply for hire for such use ;

shall apply to motor vehicles adapted to carry less than nine passengers as they apply to motor vehicles adapted to carry less than eight passengers.

The London Hackney Carriages Act 1843

2. In section 25 of the London Hackney Carriages Act 1843 (power to revoke or suspend licences of drivers of hackney carriages), the following paragraph shall be added at the end—

    " A magistrates' court that makes an order revoking or suspending any licence under this section may, if the court thinks fit, suspend the effect of the order pending an appeal against the order."

The Town Police Clauses Act 1847

3. Section 46 of the Town Police Clauses Act 1847 (drivers not to act without first obtaining a licence) shall not apply to a person driving a hackney carriage licensed under that Act for the purpose of or in connection with—

    (*a*) any test of the mechanical condition or fitness of the hackney carriage or its equipment carried out for the purposes of section 43 of the Road Traffic Act 1972 (tests of satisfactory condition of vehicles other than goods vehicles) or for the purposes of any requirements with respect to such condition or fitness imposed by or under any other enactment ; or

Sch. 7

         (b) any test of that person's competence to drive a hackney carriage carried out for the purposes of any application made by him for a licence to drive a hackney carriage.

1930 c. 43.

The Road Traffic Act 1930

4. In section 101 of the Road Traffic Act 1930 (power of local authorities to run public service vehicles), paragraph (a) of subsection (2) (exclusion of power to run such a vehicle as a contract carriage) shall be omitted.

1954 c. 64.

The Transport Charges &c. (Miscellaneous Provisions) Act 1954

5. Section 1 of the Transport Charges &c. (Miscellaneous Provisions) Act 1954 shall cease to have effect.

1962 c. 46.

The Transport Act 1962

6. In section 3(3) of the 1962 Act (powers of the Railways Board), for paragraph (b) (power to carry goods and passengers by road) there shall be substituted the following paragraph—

    " (b) in the circumstances specified in sections 4 and 4A of this Act respectively, to carry goods by road and to secure the provision by other persons of services for the carriage of passengers by road ".

1968 c. 73.

The Transport Act 1968

7. In section 10(1)(xiii) of the 1968 Act (power of Passenger Transport Executive to charge for services, etc.), after the word " Act " there shall be inserted the words " and section 104(1) of the Transport Act 1985 (travel concessions on services provided by Passenger Transport Executives) ".

8. In section 15(2)(b) of that Act (approval of Passenger Transport Authority required for reduction or waiver of charges by Executive), for the words " 138(1) of this Act " there shall be substituted the words " 104(2) of the Transport Act 1985 (travel concessions on services provided by Passenger Transport Executives) ".

9. In section 16(2) of that Act (annual report of Authorities and Executives to include information with respect to certain businesses carried on by Executives and their subsidiaries), for the words from " which do not " to " road service licence " there shall be substituted the words " other than local services ".

10. In section 34 of that Act (assistance for rural bus or ferry services), as it applies to England and Wales—

         (a) in subsection (1) the words " bus service or " shall be omitted ; and

         (b) after that subsection there shall be inserted the following subsection—

        " (1A) The Council of the Isles of Scilly may, on such conditions, if any, as they think fit, afford assistance to any other person, by way of grant, loan or both, for the purpose of securing the provision, improvement

or continuance of any bus service if in the opinion of   Sch. 7
that Council that service is or will be for the benefit
of persons residing in rural areas.".

11. In section 34 of that Act (assistance for rural bus or ferry
service), as it applies to Scotland—

    (*a*) subsection (1) ; and

    (*b*) in subsection (3), the words " (1) or " ;

shall be omitted.

12. In section 56 of that Act (assistance towards capital expenditure on public transport facilities), for subsection (4) (which excludes
grants under the section unless the grant-making authorities are
satisfied that the purpose in view accords with general transport
planning for the relevant locality) there shall be substituted the
following subsection—

    " (4) No grant under subsection (1) of this section shall be
made for any purpose unless the Secretary of State is satisfied
that the provision, improvement or development of the facilities in question is appropriate in the light of—

        (*a*) any general policies formulated by a Passenger Trans-
port Authority under section 9A(1) or (5) of this Act ;

        (*b*) any general policies formulated by a non-metro-
politan county council under section 63(1) or by a
regional or islands council under section 63(2) of the
Transport Act 1985 (policies with respect to services to
be secured to meet public transport requirements within
the county) ; and

        (*c*) any measures adopted by such a council under sub-
section (6) of that section (measures for promoting co-
ordination of services and convenience of the public
in using services for their area) ;

which are relevant to the need for facilities of the description
in question in the locality in which they are, or are to be,
provided ; and no payment under subsection (2) of this section
shall be made for any purpose unless the local authority or
local authorities in question are so satisfied."

The Post Office Act 1969   1969 c. 48.

13. Section 7 of the Post Office Act 1969 (Post Office powers),
shall be amended as follows—

    (*a*) there shall be substituted for the word " and " at the end
of subsection (1)(*e*) the words—

        " (*ee*) with the consent of, or in accordance with the
terms of a general authorisation given by, the Secretary
of State, to perform, in such parts of post offices as are
open to the public for the transaction of postal business,
such services for any operator of a public passenger
transport service (within the meaning of the Transport
Act 1985), or any subsidiary of such an operator, as it
thinks fit, being services which are connected with the
provision of public passenger transport services ; and " ;
and

(*b*) in subsection (1A)(*f*), the words from " above " to the end shall be omitted.

The Local Authority Social Services Act 1970

14. At the end of section 5(6) of the Local Authority Social Services Act 1970 (definition of " disqualified " in relation to membership of a social services committee) there shall be inserted the words " or under section 74 of the Transport Act 1985 (disabilities of directors of public transport companies) ".

The Tribunals and Inquiries Act 1971

15. In Part I of Schedule 1 to the Tribunals and Inquiries Act 1971 (tribunals under direct supervision of the Council on Tribunals), for paragraph 31 there shall be substituted the following paragraph—

" Transport.   31. The Transport Tribunal constituted as provided in Schedule 4 to the Transport Act 1985.".

The Local Government (Scotland) Act 1973

16. In Schedule 18 to the Local Government (Scotland) Act 1973, paragraphs 20, 27 and 28 shall be omitted.

The Local Government (Miscellaneous Provisions) Act 1976

17.—(1) In section 46(1)(*a*) of the Local Government (Miscellaneous Provisions) Act 1976 (prohibition on use as a private hire vehicle of a vehicle which is not a licensed hackney carriage), after the words " hackney carriage " there shall be inserted the words " or London cab ".

(2) In section 75(1) of that Act (vehicles to which Part II does not apply), the following paragraph shall be inserted after paragraph (*c*)—

" (*cc*) apply to a vehicle while it is being used in connection with a wedding ; "

and paragraph (*d*)(i) shall be omitted.

(3) In section 80(1) of that Act (interpretation of Part II)—

(*a*) the following definition shall be inserted at the appropriate place—

" " London cab " means a vehicle which is a hackney carriage within the meaning of the Metropolitan Public Carriage Act 1869 ; " ;

(*b*) in the definition of " private hire vehicle ", after the words " service vehicle " there shall be inserted the words " or a London cab " ; and

(*c*) in the definition of " vehicle licence ", after the words " the Act of 1847 " there shall be inserted the words " in relation to a London cab a licence under section 6 of the Metropolitan Public Carriage Act 1869 ".

The Licensing (Scotland) Act 1976

18. In section 92 of the Licensing (Scotland) Act 1976 (restriction on the carriage of alcoholic liquor on contract carriages)—

(*a*) in subsection (1), there shall be substituted for the words

"public service vehicle licence" the words "PSV operator's licence" and for the words "as a contract carriage"
the words "for the carriage of passengers otherwise than at
separate fares";

(b) in subsection (3), there shall be substituted for the words
"public service vehicle licence" the words "PSV operator's
licence"; and

(c) for subsection (5) there shall be substituted the following
subsection—

"(5) In this section "PSV operator's licence" has the
like meaning as in Part II of the Public Passenger Vehicles
Act 1981."

The Concessionary Travel for Handicapped Persons (Scotland) Act 1980

19.—(1) In section 1 of the Concessionary Travel for Handicapped
Persons (Scotland) Act 1980 (travel concessions for handicapped
persons)—

(a) subsection (1) shall be omitted; and

(b) for subsection (2) there shall be substituted the following
subsection—

"(2) Section 93 of the Transport Act 1985 (travel concession schemes) shall apply in relation to handicapped
persons as it applies in relation to persons mentioned in
subsection (7) of that section.".

(2) In section 2(1) of that Act (interpretation)—

(a) in the definition of "handicapped persons", for the words
from "qualified" to "1964" there shall be substituted the
words "eligible persons within the meaning of section 93(7)
of the Transport Act 1985";

(b) the definition of "public service vehicle" shall be omitted;
and

(c) in the definition of "travel concession", for the word
"1955" there shall be substituted the word "1985".

The Transport Act 1980

20. In section 64(3) of the Transport Act 1980 (definition of taxi),
for the words "section 270 of the Burgh Police (Scotland) Act
1892" there shall be substituted the words "section 10 of the Civic
Government (Scotland) Act 1982".

The Public Passenger Vehicles Act 1981

21. (1) The Public Passenger Vehicles Act 1981 shall be amended
as follows.

(2) In section 8 (powers of inspection, including rights of entry, in
relation to public service vehicles), after subsection (1) there shall be
inserted the following subsection—

"(1A) For the purposes of subsection (1)(b) above, a vehicle
which is used to carry passengers for hire or reward only under
a permit granted under section 19 or 22 of the Transport Act
1985 (permits relating to the use of vehicles by educational and

other bodies or in providing community bus services) shall be treated as not being a public service vehicle.".

(3) In section 9 (power to prohibit driving of unfit public service vehicles), in subsection (8), after the word "examiner", in the second place where it occurs, there shall be inserted the words " or certifying officer " and for the words " by a certifying officer and " there shall be substituted—

　　" (*a*) in the case of a refusal by a public service vehicle examiner, by a certifying officer ; and

　　(*b*) in the case of a refusal by a certifying officer, by another certifying officer ;
and ".

(4) In section 16(1), there shall be inserted at the beginning " Subject to subsection (1A) below and section 12(7) of the Transport Act 1985 ".

(5) In section 17(3) (grounds for the revocation, suspension, etc., of a PSV operator's licence by a traffic commissioner), there shall be added at the end—

　　" (*f*) the licence is one in relation to which a direction given by a traffic commissioner under section 28(4) of the Transport Act 1985 (power when disqualifying a former licence holder to direct that certain other PSV operators' licences should be liable to be revoked, suspended, etc.) has effect ".

(6) In section 17(4) (traffic commissioners not to take action under section 17(1) or (2) without first holding public sitting) for the words " a public sitting " there shall be substituted the words " an inquiry ".

(7) In section 22(2) (person to whom application for public service vehicle driver licence to be made), for paragraphs (*a*) and (*b*) there shall be substituted the words " the traffic commissioner for the traffic area in which that person resides at the time when he applies for a licence ".

(8) In section 56(1) (records of licences, etc.), there shall be added at the end, the words " and shall allow the record to be inspected at all reasonable times by members of the public ".

(9) In section 60 (power to make regulations), in subsection (1)(*f*) after the word " by " there shall be inserted the words ", and the information to be displayed in or on ", and at the end there shall be added the words " or it is to be displayed ".

(10) In section 79 (vehicles excluded from regulation as private hire vehicles), for the words " or 42(1) " there shall be substituted the words " or (4) ".

(11) In section 87 (power to repeal specified sections of the Act), for the reference to " 50(6)(*b*) " there shall be substituted a reference to " 51(1)(*b*) ".

(12) In Schedule 1 (conditions affecting status or classification as a public service vehicle), paragraph 4 (parties of overseas visitors) shall cease to have effect.

The Local Government Finance Act 1982

22.—(1) In section 31 of the Local Government Finance Act 1982 (Passenger Transport Executives and their subsidiaries), for subsection (4) (power of Secretary of State to apply Part III of that Act to subsidiaries of Executives) there shall be substituted the following subsection—

" (4) Where a Passenger Transport Executive have a subsidiary, it shall be their duty to exercise their control over that subsidiary so as to ensure that the subsidiary appoints only auditors who, in addition to being qualified for appointment as such auditors in accordance with section 389 of the Com- panies Act 1985, are approved by the Commission for appointment as auditors of that subsidiary."

(2) In subsection (6) of that section, for the words from " the company " to the end there shall be substituted the words " subsection (4) above shall not apply, but it shall be the joint duty of the Executive and the other body or bodies concerned to exercise such control over the company as the Executive are required by that subsection to exercise over a subsidiary of theirs.".

(3) In section 36(1) of that Act (interpretation of Part III), in the definition of " auditor ", after the word " means " there shall be inserted the words " (except in section 31(4) above) ".

The Civic Government (Scotland) Act 1982

23.—(1) The Civic Government (Scotland) Act 1982 shall be amended as follows.

(2) In section 18(6) (power of Secretary of State to make rules as to procedure in relation to appeals in respect of taxi fares), after the word " may " there shall be inserted the words " by order made by statutory instrument ".

(3) In section 20(1) (regulations relating to taxis and private hire cars and their drivers), at the end there shall be added the words—

" and may provide that such conditions shall be imposed or, as the case may be, shall not be imposed for different areas or classes of areas ; and different conditions or classes of conditions may be prescribed in relation to different categories of taxi or private hire car."

(4) In section 21(2) (offences), after the word " driver " where second occurring there shall be inserted the words—

" (otherwise than in a public place from the person to be conveyed in it, or a person acting on his behalf, for a journey beginning there and then) ".

(5) In section 10 (taxi and private hire car licences), for subsection (3) (refusal to grant taxi licences) there shall be substituted the following subsection—

" (3) Without prejudice to paragraph 5 of Schedule 1 to this Act, the grant of a taxi licence may be refused by a licensing authority for the purpose of limiting the number of taxis in

SCH. 7
respect of which licences are granted by them if, but only if, they are satisfied that there is no significant demand for the services of taxis in their area which is unmet."

1984 c. 32.

The London Regional Transport Act 1984

24. In section 35(1) of the London Regional Transport Act 1984 (application of section to certain businesses carried on by London Regional Transport or any subsidiary of theirs), for the words from " which do not " to the end there shall be substituted the words " other than local services (within the meaning of the Transport Act 1985) ".

25. In section 55(3) of that Act (definitions of expressions used in the penalty fares provisions), for the definition of " bus service " there shall be substituted the following—

" " bus service " means a local service within the meaning of the Transport Act 1985 other than an excursion or tour within the meaning of that Act ; ".

26. In section 68 of that Act (interpretation), the definitions of " London bus service " and "road service licence " shall be omitted.

27. In Schedule 5 to that Act (transitional provisions and savings)—

(*a*) at the end of paragraph 10 there shall be added the following sub-paragraph—

" (9) In this paragraph and paragraphs 11 and 12 below—

(*a*) " London bus service " has the same meaning as in Part II of the Transport Act 1985 ; and

(*b*) " London local service licence " means a London local service licence under that Part of that Act." ;

(*b*) for the word " road ", in each place where it occurs in paragraphs 11 and 12, there shall be substituted the words " London local " ;

(*c*) in paragraph 11(4) the words from " (and shall accordingly " to the end shall be omitted ;

1981 c. 14.

(*d*) in paragraph 12(3), for the words " the Public Passenger Vehicles Act 1981 " there shall be substituted the words " Part II of the Transport Act 1985 " ;

(*e*) in paragraph 12(4), for the words " 31(2) to (4), 34 and 35 " there shall be substituted the words " 37(2) and (3) and 39 " ;

(*f*) in paragraph 12(5), for " 32(1) " there shall be substituted the words " 38(1) and (2) " and for the words " subsection (5) " there shall be substituted the words " subsections (6) and (7) " ;

(*g*) paragraph 12(6) shall be omitted ; and

(*h*) in paragraph 12(7), for " 37(2) " there shall be substituted " 41(1) ".

SCHEDULE 8

REPEALS

Chapter	Short title	Extent of repeal
10 & 11 Vict. c. 89.	The Town Police Clauses Act 1847.	In section 37, the words " such number of " and " as they think fit ".
20 & 21 Geo. 5. c. 43.	The Road Traffic Act 1930.	In section 101(2), paragraph (*a*). In section 121(1A), the words " contract carriages ".
2 & 3 Eliz. 2. c. 64.	The Transport Charges &c. (Miscellaneous Provisions) Act 1954.	Section 1. In section 12, in subsection (1), the words from " including " to "Act " and subsection (2). In section 13(1), the words " public service vehicles, road service licences and ".
3 & 4 Eliz. 2. c. 26.	The Public Service Vehicles (Travel Concessions) Act 1955.	The whole Act.
10 & 11 Eliz. 2. c. 46.	The Transport Act 1962.	In section 4, in subsection (1)(*a*), the word " and " immediately following sub-paragraph (ii), sub-paragraph (iii) and the words " and passengers ", subsection (5), and in subsection (6) the words " or passengers ". Section 57, except subsection (7). In section 92, the definitions of the following expressions— "contract carriage"; "express carriage "; and " stage carriage ". Schedule 10.
1964 c. 95.	The Travel Concessions Act 1964.	The whole Act.
1965 c. 25.	The Finance Act 1965.	In section 92(1), the words " any bus service ".
1968 c. 73.	The Transport Act 1968.	In section 9, in subsection (6) the words " or 6 ", and subsection (7). In section 10(2), the words from " or with the consent " to "Act ". Section 11(1), as it applies to England and Wales. In section 12(3)(*d*), the words from " or by " to the end of the paragraph. In section 14(3), as it applies to Scotland, the words " for the designated area ". In section 15, subsection (1)(*a*), in subsection (2)(*a*) the words from " or provided by " to "Act ", subsection (3) and— (*a*) in relation to England and

SCH. 8

Chapter	Short title	Extent of repeal
1968 c. 73. —*cont.*	The Transport Act 1968 —*cont.*	Wales, the words in sub-section (2) following paragraph (*b*) and subsection (4); and (*b*) in relation to Scotland, the words in subsection (2) from " and, in the case " to the end. Section 15A(1). In section 16(2), the words from " and if " to " would not ". Sections 17 to 19. In section 20, subsection (1), in subsection (2) the words " to which this section applies " and in paragraph (*a*) the words " review as soon as may be, and subsequently ", and subsection (8). Section 21. In section 22, in subsections (1) and (2) the words " or regulations ", and subsections (3) to (6). Section 24(3). Section 29(4). In section 34(1) as it applies to England and Wales, the words " bus service or ". In section 34, as it applies to Scotland, subsection (1) and, in subsection (3), the words " (1) or ". Section 36. In section 54, in subsection (5)(*d*) the words from " and to the Bus Company " to " Scottish Group ", and in the words following paragraph (*d*) the words from " or, where " to " jointly " and the words from " or, as the case may be " to the end, and subsection (6). Section 59(3). Section 88. Section 90. In section 103(1), the definition of " licensing authority ". Section 138. In section 159(1), the definitions of the following expressions— " area bus service "; " excursion or tour "; " express carriage " and " stage carriage "; and " road service licence ".

Chapter	Short title	Extent of repeal
1968 c. 73.— *cont.*	The Transport Act 1968 —*cont.*	In Schedule 5— Part I; in Part II, paragraph 1; and in Part III— paragraphs 1, 2, 3(*a*), 4, 5, 10, 11(*c*), 12, 16 and 17; in paragraphs 6, 7 and 9, the words " the Authority and " and " respectively " in each place where they occur; in paragraph 8, the words " the Authority or " and " the chairman of the Authority or, as the case may be "; in paragraph 11, in sub-paragraph (*a*), the words " the Authority or " and in sub-paragraph (*b*), the words " the Authority "; and in paragraph 13, the words " the Authority or ", in both places where they occur, and " the Authority " where those words last occur. Schedule 6. In Part II of Schedule 10, the entries relating to the Transport Act 1962.
1969 c. 48.	The Post Office Act 1969.	In section 7(1A)(*f*), the words from " above " to the end.
1970 c. 24.	The Finance Act 1970.	Section 16(1).
1972 c. 70.	The Local Government Act 1972.	Section 80(4). Section 186(5). In section 202, subsection (1), the words " Subject to subsection (3) below " in subsection (2) and subsections (3) to (7). In Schedule 24, Part II.
1973 c. 65.	The Local Government (Scotland) Act 1973.	Section 150(5). Section 151. In Schedule 18, paragraphs 1(*a*) to (*d*) and (*f*), 7(*c*), 10, 11, 20, 21(1), 27 and 28.
1974 c. 7.	The Local Government Act 1974.	In Schedule 6, paragraph 22(7).
1976 c. 76.	The Energy Act 1976.	In Schedule 1, in paragraph 1(1)(*c*) the words " or Part III " and " and ", paragraph 1(1)(*d*) and in paragraph 1(2) the words " section 60 of " and the words from "general" to first " vehicles ".

Chapter	Short title	Extent of repeal
1978 c. 55.	The Transport Act 1978.	Sections 1 to 4.
1980 c. 29.	The Concessionary Travel for Handicapped Persons (Scotland) Act 1980.	Section 1(1). In section 2(1), the definition of " public service vehicle ".
1980 c. 34.	The Transport Act 1980.	In Schedule 5, in Part II, the paragraph amending the Transport Act 1968.
1980 c. 65.	The Local Government, Planning and Land Act 1980.	In section 4(4)(*e*), the words from " established " to the end. In section 82, in subsection (1)(*a*) the words " whose area is either the whole or part of one county ", and subsections (2) and (3).
1981 c. 14.	The Public Passenger Vehicles Act 1981.	In section 1, in subsection (3) the word " II " and in subsection (5) the words " section 2 ". Section 2. In section 16(8), the words " under this section ". Section 28. Part III. Sections 42 to 45. In section 46, in subsection (1)(*b*) the word " bus " (where it occurs in " local bus service "), and in subsection (3) the definition of " local bus service ". Sections 47 to 49. In section 52(1)(*a*)(i), the words " and road service licences ". In section 52(3), the words " or by virtue of regulations under section 44 of this Act ". In section 53(1), the word " the " before the words " traffic commissioners " and the words " or section 45 ". In section 56, in subsection (1) the words " them or " and subsection (2). In section 57, the words " or road service licence " (in each place where they occur). In section 58(2), the words " or road service licence ". In section 59, in paragraph (*a*) the words " road service licences ", and in paragraph (*b*) the words " or road service licences ".

Chapter	Short title	Extent of repeal
1981 c. 14.— *cont.*	The Public Passenger Vehicles Act. 1981.— *cont.*	In section 60— in subsection (1), the words from "for any purpose" to "generally", the words from "and regulations under this section" to the end, paragraph (*d*) and in paragraph (*h*) the words "or, as the case may be, the commissioner of police of the metropolis"; and subsection (3). In section 61(2), the words "section 59 or 60 of". Section 62. In section 65(1)(*a*), the words "or III". In section 66(*a*), the words "or III". In section 67, the words "other than regulations made under section 44 thereof". In section 68, in subsection (2) the words "33(7), 40(6)". In section 69(1), the words "or III". In section 70(1), the words "or III". In section 71(1), the words "or III". In section 72, the words "or III". In section 74(1), the words "or Part III". In section 76, the words from "except" to the end. Section 81(2). In section 82(1), the definitions of the following expressions— "community bus service"; "contract carriage"; "excursion or tour"; "express carriage" and "express carriage service"; "road service licence"; "stage carriage" and "stage carriage service"; and "trial area". In section 83, in subsection (1) the words "" stage carriage", "express carriage" or "contract carriage"", and subsection (2). In Schedule 1, paragraphs **3** and **4**. Schedule 4. Schedule 5.

SCH. 8

Chapter	Short Title	Extent of Repeal
1982 c. 49.	The Transport Act 1982.	Part I. In section 73(4), the words " 5(5) or ".
1983 c. 10.	The Transport Act 1983.	In section 3, in subsection (1) the word " and " immediately following paragraph (*a*), and in subsection (4) the word " and " immediately following paragraph (*b*). Section 9(2).
1984 c. 27.	The Road Traffic Regulation Act 1984.	Section 3(4). In Schedule 13, paragraphs 48 and 49.
1984 c. 32.	The London Regional Transport Act 1984.	In section 28, in subsection (1) paragraph (*d*) and the word " or " immediately preceding it, and in subsection (2) the words " and the council of any district ". Sections 43 to 45. In section 50, subsections (2) and (6) and, in subsection (8)(*a*), sub-paragraph (i) and the words from " and any person " to the end of the paragraph. In section 68, the definitions of " London bus service " and " road service licence ". In Schedule 5, in paragraph 11(4) the words from " (and shall accordingly " to the end, and paragraph 12(6). In Schedule 6, paragraphs 3, 5, 6 and 15(1)(*a*).
1985 c. 51.	The Local Government Act 1985.	In section 42(1)(*c*), the words " which is or was coterminous with a metropolitan county '. In Schedule 12, paragraphs 1, 2, 3(2) and 4. In Schedule 14, paragraph 59(1)(*e*).

PRINTED IN ENGLAND BY W. J. SHARP, CB
Controller and Chief Executive of Her Majesty's Stationery Office and
Queen's Printer of Acts of Parliament

(546753)